THE
DEPRESSION
ANSWER BOOK™

Professional Answers to More Than 275 Critical Questions About Medication, Therapy, Support & More

THE DEPRESSION ANSWER BOOK™

Professional Answers to More Than 275 Critical Questions About Medication, Therapy, Support & More

— WES BURGESS, MD, PhD —

SOURCEBOOKS, INC.®
NAPERVILLE, ILLINOIS

Published by Sourcebooks, Inc.
P.O. Box 4410, Naperville, Illinois 60567-4410
(630) 961-3900
Fax: (630) 961-2168
www.sourcebooks.com

Library of Congress Cataloging-in-Publication Data

Burgess, Wes.
  The depression answer book : professional answers to more than 275 critical questions about medication, therapy, support, and more / by Wes Burgess.
        p. cm.
1. Depression, Mental—Popular works. 2. Depression, Mental—Miscellanea. I. Title.
  RC537.B868 2009
  616.85'27—dc22
                                2008048510

Printed and bound in the United States of America.
UGI 10 9 8 7 6 5 4 3 2 1

Contents

Prologue

Wake up to find out that you are the eyes of the world.
The heart has its beaches, its homeland, and thoughts of its own.
Wake now, discover that you are the song that the morning brings.
The heart has its seasons, its evenings, and songs of its own.

Introduction

If you or someone you know suffers from depression, *don't give up hope!* This book will help you understand depression and give you proven, practical solutions that have helped people triumph over their depression and take back their lives.

Depressed patients and their families and friends tell me that they have looked everywhere for the answers to their most important questions about fighting this illness. They have looked in bookstores and online; asked their doctors and therapists; called, texted, and emailed their friends. They found contradictory information, preachy jargon, and stories about depressive misery, but they did *not* find the answers they needed.

My patients asked me to write *The Depression Answer Book* so they could take the book home to read and reread and share with their families and friends. My patients' friends, significant others, marriage partners, children, and parents asked me for a book that explains how to help the depressed person in their lives. Doctors, nurses, and psychotherapists asked me to write a book that they could give to their depressed patients and their families to help answer their questions.

Ever since I started my psychiatric practice twenty years ago, I have been writing down the questions asked by my depressed patients, their families, and their friends. I have scoured the Internet to find questions on depression that were left unanswered, and I picked the brains of other doctors and therapists to find out what questions their patients asked them. *The Depression Answer Book* is a collection of these real-life questions with answers drawn from the most current scientific, medical, and psychological knowledge, combined with my own clinical experience. I am sure that you will find the answers to *your* important questions here.

I began my professional life as a scientist, studying behavior and the brain in the departments of medicine and psychology at major universities. Twenty years ago, I felt a calling to go to clinical work so I could spend the rest of my life helping people with unipolar major depression and other illnesses. I completed my specialty training at Stanford University Medical School and served as a fellow at Stanford University and UCLA medical schools. Since then, as a licensed medical doctor, practicing psychiatrist, and psychotherapist, I have worked every day to help depressed people find their way back to their normal lives.

I wrote *The Depression Answer Book* in such a way that it feels as if you and I are sitting down and talking face-to-face; as if I'm giving you individual counsel and cutting-edge information on the topics that you choose. This book contains detailed, up-to-the-minute information, yet I want it to be easy to read and understand.

I want *The Depression Answer Book* to provide practical answers for seemingly insolvable problems, and I hope that this book helps you free yourself from your depression forever. I want you to have information that will allow you to make the best choices for you, and to help you guide your own treatment so you get what you want from your doctor and therapist. I want you and your loved ones to feel better by understanding depression and knowing what to do about it. I can hardly wait to get started. Let's not waste any more time.

Chapter 1

DEPRESSION BASICS

- What's a simple definition of major depression?
- Is major depression a medical disease or just a bad attitude?
- Is depression a fad diagnosis?
- How many people are affected by clinical depression?
- Does depression cause physical problems?
- How does being seriously depressed affect my overall health?
- How serious is my depression?
- Who is most likely to have an episode of major depression?
- Does major depression get worse over time?
- Will I have to keep taking medications or going to psychotherapy for the rest of my life?
- How does depression affect people's longevity?
- Is there any good news about this diagnosis?

What's a simple definition of major depression?

Major depression is a condition of the brain and nervous system that causes a loss of both pleasure and interest in life. It is usually characterized by sadness, pessimism, and hopelessness. However, depression is more than just a change in emotions; it is a real medical illness with physical symptoms such as disturbed sleep, loss of appetite, change in weight, decreased energy, slowness, and difficulty focusing.

Is major depression a medical disease or just a bad attitude?

Medical, biological, and psychological factors are all at work in major depression. The physical symptoms—mental slowing, poor concentration, intrusive thoughts, disturbed sleep, change in appetite, decreased energy, decreased sexual interest, body pain, and disrupted body rhythms—demonstrate that depression is a physical process. The depressive thoughts of pessimism, worry, self-criticism, distortion, and death are clearly psychological.

It is unfortunate that the word "depression" is used to describe both a medical disease and a bad mood. Some people confuse the two and think that the significant physical, mental, and emotional deterioration caused by major depression is no more serious than a bad mood. Anyone who has suffered from the disease of major depression knows that there is little similarity between the two.

This linguistic mix-up contributes to some myths surrounding major depression. After all, if you're just in a bad mood, people wonder why you cannot exert some effort and pull yourself out of it. However, you usually cannot pull yourself out of major depression; it can be severely debilitating and too often results in death by accident or suicide. People do not kill themselves because they are in a bad mood.

There are even other, different medical conditions that have the word "depression" in the title, like bipolar depression, organic depression, etc. To keep everything straight, in this book we will often use the correct term "unipolar major depression" so there is no question of what we mean.

Is depression a fad diagnosis?

Major depression has been recognized by physicians since the beginning of written medicine, and during that time, depression symptoms have not changed. The Greek godfather of medicine, Hippocrates (who authored the Hippocratic Oath sworn by most doctors), described major depression symptoms in 400 BC: sleeplessness, despondency, irritability, restlessness, and an aversion to food. One of the first English-language books on depression was published in 1621 (*The Anatomy of Melancholy* by Robert Burton). Depression is no trendy diagnosis; we have known about it and been aware of its seriousness for a long time.

How many people are affected by clinical depression?

Every year major depression affects well over 18 million people, 6 percent of the total population of the United States. Counting spouses, significant others, parents, children, grandparents, doctors, nurses, psychotherapists, and friends, depression touches the lives of about 200 million people in the United States right now. These figures are similar for other developed countries.

Does depression cause physical problems?

Major depression can disrupt the normal functions of your body, causing decreased sexual interest and hormonal changes, as well as an increase in headaches, joint pain, muscle pain, stomachaches, and digestive problems. Major depression alters the biochemistry of your brain, and every episode of depression makes the illness worse. Your thoughts are slowed, your concentration is impaired, and intrusive thoughts come into your mind and repeat over and over.

Your mind is taken over by worries, self-criticism, guilt, and thoughts of death. During an episode of major depression, your perception of the world is distorted. Good situations look worse than they are, and bad situations look hopeless. Wherever you look, there is no satisfaction and no peace from your dark, negative emotions and thoughts.

How does being seriously depressed affect my overall health?

Individuals with major depression are more likely to have asthma, arthritis, and diabetes than the rest of the population. Depression is just as important a risk factor for heart disease as smoking and high blood pressure. When individuals suffering from heart failure have a depressed episode, it increases their likelihood of dying by 15 percent. In contrast, studies show that after their depression is treated with antidepressants, survivors of heart attacks are less likely to have another heart attack.

If you have several episodes of depression, you are more likely to develop dementia. Studies have shown that depression frequently precedes Alzheimer's disease. Fortunately, depressed people are much less likely to have health problems if they get appropriate treatment like antidepressants and psychotherapy. When your depression has been effectively treated with antidepressant medications and psychotherapy, you will look, act, and feel just like anyone else, if not better. And treatment is successful in the vast majority of cases.

How serious is my depression?

The emotional and physical pain, social isolation, poor concentration, and bad decision-making brought on by unipolar major depression can cause you to lose the things you value most. Individuals suffering from depression frequently end up destroying important relationships with wives, husbands, girlfriends, boyfriends, parents, children, and friends. Depression causes people to fail at work and school, lose their jobs, deplete their savings, and become unable to take care of their personal responsibilities. In the workplace, depression is the second leading cause of disability in the world, creating problems for individuals, coworkers, corporations, and national economies. Depression is a big deal—it's crucial to seek treatment.

Who is most likely to have an episode of major depression?

Individuals thirty to forty years of age are most likely to get their first major depressive episode, although depression can also show up in children and the elderly. Depression is diagnosed in about twice as many women as men, though some of this difference may result from men's reluctance to seek treatment.

By far, the people most likely to have unipolar depressive episodes are those individuals who have had an episode in the past. This is why the goals of depression treatment are to eliminate your symptoms now *and* prevent any more depression in the future.

Does major depression get worse over time?

Every time you have an episode of unipolar major depression, your illness gets worse and harder to treat. For example, after the first episode, you have a 50 percent chance of getting depressed again within the next year after treatment is stopped. After you've had two episodes, the likelihood of having another one increases to

70 percent. If you have three episodes of depression, you have a 90 percent chance of having another recurrence. Studies suggest that every depressed episode increases the death of brain cells and turns off the brain's natural protection system. This is why it is so important to make sure that no further episodes occur.

Will I have to keep taking medications or going to psychotherapy for the rest of my life?

You can stop your treatment anytime you want; it's up to you. However, the risk of having another depressive episode that could damage work, school, family, and social life is very high, and many people choose to continue their treatment even after they've stabilized. In particular, continuing to take antidepressants will protect your brain cells from stress damage and keep your depression from becoming more severe. Many experts suggest that after two or more episodes (when the risk of recurrence is 70 percent or more), patients should consider staying on their antidepressants indefinitely.

However, that is not the whole story. Every year we have better treatments for unipolar major depression, and you'll continue to have more and better options as research moves forward. If you choose to continue your current treatment, it will not be long before you have better options to select from. I believe that, not too far in the future, we will find a way to alter the underlying genetic code with one treatment that will keep you free of depression for life.

The preventative benefits of psychotherapy are less clear. It has been proven that the right types of psychotherapy can keep depression from returning for months. We do not yet have sufficient research to know if psychotherapy can prevent later depression episodes.

How does depression affect people's longevity?

The pain of untreated depression is often so terrible that some sufferers would rather end their lives than continue to live through the torment. About 15 percent of people with unipolar major depression will attempt suicide each year, and about 15 percent of them will succeed. (This only includes the fraction of people whose deaths are reported as suicide.) The lifetime risk for suicide is higher in unipolar major depression than in schizophrenia or panic disorder—depression is a potentially fatal illness.

Recent estimates suggest that the mortality from depression is second only to cancer in some areas. In addition to suicide, if we add in all the fatalities from motor vehicle crashes, falls, poisoning, and other accidents that accompany depression, the number of depression deaths is much higher.

Is there any good news about this diagnosis?

The good news is that, with the right treatment, you will get over this episode and may never have to be depressed again! About 60–80 percent of depressed people who take antidepressants get better, and that percentage increases when psychotherapy is added. So while depression is a serious diagnosis for which you need treatment, there are many reasons to hope for a full recovery.

Chapter 2

SYMPTOMS OF DEPRESSION

■ What do people look like when they are depressed?

■ What kind of emotional changes can I expect if my depression grows worse?

■ I can't seem to eat—what's wrong with my appetite?

■ Why do I always binge on junk food and put on weight when I get depressed?

■ Why do I never seem to get any restful sleep?

■ Can I take antidepressants to give myself more energy?

■ What physical symptoms are typical with serious depression?

■ Why do my thoughts and movements feel like they've slowed down?

■ Is indecisiveness a symptom of depression?

■ Was my depression caused by recent disappointments and failures?

■ It seems like the way I think is different now that I am depressed. Could this be true?

■ What should I do if I am feeling suicidal?

■ How can I gauge the severity of my depression and understand how it changes over time?

■ All this information seems overwhelming—what can I do to fight all these problems?

What do people look like when they are depressed?

You can usually learn a lot about someone's feelings by their appearance and behavior. Depressed individuals often talk slowly, move slowly, and gesture less than they did before. They may hang their heads or have difficulty looking you in the eyes when you speak to them. When people begin to develop unipolar major depression, they often start wearing dark or drab-colored clothing. They may lose weight, and their clothes will drape around their thin frames.

In close quarters, depressed individuals often go out of their way to avoid touching other people, tending to sit at a distance with crossed arms and legs that signify "keep away." They might also draw in their arms and legs and sink into the couch or chair until they almost seem to be shrinking.

Fortunately, these tendencies go away with successful treatment, and you'll see their appearance return to normal as the depression lifts.

What kind of emotional changes can I expect if my depression grows worse?

Negative emotions like sadness, anxiety, loneliness, irritability, fear, anger, and panic grow stronger and are easier to trigger as your depressive episode progresses. For example, you may have watched some of your favorite movies for years and thoroughly enjoyed them every time. Now that you are depressed, you find yourself sad and crying at the same scenes you laughed at before.

You may also lose access to your usual range of emotions. People suffering from unipolar major depression often find that their emotions become restricted to just a few feelings, negative ones such as sadness, anger, and despair. For example, it may be your birthday and you're surrounded by happy people, presents, ice cream, and cake. Despite the joyful environment, you cannot find those happy emotions that you know you should be having.

Your senses could be dulled, and you might withdraw into yourself, feeling numb and empty. For example, you may be watching a ball game, a pursuit that you have always enjoyed in the past. Now, you do not seem to be able to focus on the game, who is playing, or what the score is. You feel like you are way up in the bleachers, looking down on something small and far away. Later that night, listening to your friends discussing the game, you have the same feeling, as if you're separated from them by a thick pane of glass.

The worst part of depression treatment can be the realization that you'll have to wait and work for your feelings to become normal and natural again. But with the right treatment and some work on your part, these unnatural emotions will pass sooner than you think.

I can't seem to eat—what's wrong with my appetite?

The physiological effects of unipolar major depression often make people lose their appetites and drop weight. It may be difficult for you to eat, because food just does not look appetizing. If you try to force yourself to eat, it might seem tasteless and unappealing. Some people with major depressive illness find the very thought of food nauseating.

In our weight-conscious society, you may be happy to lose a few pounds at first, but the longer you continue to be depressed, the more weight you lose. It may not be obvious at first, but if your weight loss is extreme, other people will begin to notice that you appear drawn, sallow, and sickly. Fortunately, you will be back to your healthy self again after successful treatment.

Why do I always binge on junk food and put on weight when I get depressed?

Depression can make healthy food unappetizing until only junk food and chocolate seem attractive. If junk food is all you can get yourself to eat, you may experience excessive weight gain. Do not worry; your appetite for healthy food will return with depression treatment.

When your weight is changing, it is hard to know how much is too much. The American Psychiatric Association criteria suggest that loss or gain of more than 5 percent of your natural body weight may be caused by unipolar major depression. Your doctor can tell you more.

Why do I never seem to get any restful sleep?

Unipolar major depression affects your central nervous system so that you sleep abnormally. Typically, you may find it hard to get to sleep at night, and you may spend thirty minutes or more tossing and turning. In the morning you are likely to wake early without being able to go back to sleep. And even when you do get to sleep, your normal stages of light sleep, dreaming (REM) sleep, and deep (slow-wave) sleep are disrupted, so that your sleep is not restful. When you wake up in the morning, you are just as tired as when you went to bed.

It may be hard to relax when you are lying in bed, and you may be bombarded with thoughts about the day, your life situation, and your own self-doubts and deprecation. Taking prescription or drugstore sleeping pills can sometimes help knock you out, but most sleeping pills further upset your sleep stages. Some people try drinking alcohol to get to sleep. This appears to provide some relief at first, but this strategy eventually causes sleep to grow worse. Fortunately, antidepressants and stress-reduction techniques can help quell your intrusive thoughts, and some antidepressants can even normalize the stages of your sleep so you can get more restful sleep right away.

Can I take antidepressants to give myself more energy?

Antidepressants only help individuals who have unipolar major depression. If fatigue is the primary thing that is bothering you, try exercising more. Go to your family doctor or internist and ask for a physical examination with special attention to causes of fatigue. Fatigue alone may be caused by some internal medical problems, so get a clean bill of health before you jump into any psychiatric treatment.

What physical symptoms are typical with serious depression?

During episodes of unipolar major depression, you are more likely to experience headaches, neckaches, backaches, shoulder pain, muscle pain, and joint pain. Stomachaches, nausea, cramping, and diarrhea occur more frequently in individuals suffering from unipolar major depression.

Pain problems probably result from the increased level of inflammation that occurs during the course of unipolar major depression (see Chapter 3, Diagnosis and Causes). Physical problems usually go away as your depression begins to lift after effective treatment.

Why do my thoughts and movements feel like they've slowed down?

Slowing is a characteristic of unipolar major depression that you can feel and others around you can see. Time seems to be dragging along, and the act of thinking feels like wading through molasses. Anything you try to do seems to take forever. Others may notice that you walk slowly, talk slowly, and even drive more slowly than usual. Overall activity is decreased, and like Winston Churchill, you prefer to stand instead of walk and sit instead of stand.

In part, this slowing and loss of energy results from damage to your brain cells and insufficient amounts of the natural neurochemicals that allow your brain to function normally (see Chapter 3, Diagnosis and Causes). Fortunately, antidepressants reverse brain cell damage and increase your natural neurochemicals, while psychotherapy and relaxation techniques can reduce the stress that is driving your depression, so that you have some energy again.

Is indecisiveness a symptom of depression?

Depression causes mental slowing , and decision making can seem to take forever. In addition, depressed individuals often lack persistence and give up too easily when faced with difficult problems. Unipolar major depression may interfere with your ability to focus, making it harder to follow one train of thought before another thought intrudes, and you lose your concentration.

Depressed people should consider putting off important decisions until their depressive episode is over and their thoughts are free of the influence of unipolar major depression.

Was my depression caused by recent disappoint- ments and failures?

It's possible—having a bad year could have created the stress that pushed you into a serious bout of depression. However, it is also possible that your depression started first and is part of the reason you experienced these disappointments and failures. Have you usually made good decisions in the past? If it seems like you have not been yourself recently, maybe you were suffering from unipolar major depression for longer than you think.

In any case, the important thing to do now is to focus on your treatment so you can escape these disappointments and get back to your usual life again.

It seems like the way I think is different now that I am depressed. Could this be true?

Unipolar major depression does change the way you think, and understanding these changes can help you return your mind to its nondepressed state. For example, unipolar major depression can make you continue to think on and on about a problem until you have made a mountain out of a molehill. Your thinking is biased toward the negative, and the more you think, the more negative your thoughts become. For example, you might start watching a beautiful lake that elicits calm, peaceful thoughts. However, if you go on to think too much, you realize that the lake could be polluted, that it could carry disease, that it could overflow and kill everyone in the surrounding area. Depression has made you think too far in a negative direction until you turned a peaceful lake into a national disaster.

In addition, the negative thoughts of depression may intrude into your consciousness and repeat themselves like a broken record. Out of nowhere, your mind is drawn to your saddest, most negative memories. Long-gone memories of losses, failures, and disappointments are dredged up, and it feels like you are being forced to experience them all over again. For example, you might be working happily or watching an enjoyable film when you are suddenly distracted by lucid memories of the funeral of a loved one that you attended as a child but had not thought about for years.

In unipolar major depression, negative thoughts gradually crowd out happy thoughts until only the dark ones are left. Even if you start out with bright, positive thoughts, your depression can turn them around until you are focused on past failures, inadequacies, social faux pas, and thoughts of worthlessness. These intrusive negative thoughts can become so severe that you are convinced that you are a hopelessly flawed person who does not deserve to be happy.

If this is you, you need to go to a doctor to see if you have unipolar major depression. If you have it, you should begin appropriate treatment right away. As your depression improves with treatment, you will realize that you are really a nice person doing your best to keep afloat in the face of a serious disease, and soon you will not be able to find these dark thoughts anymore.

What should I do if I am feeling suicidal?

If you are having thoughts of suicide, be sure that your doctor and therapist know, and tell at least one other person, preferably someone who lives with you or is close by. This will help ensure that you have people to turn to for support if you begin to feel desperate.

The Journal of the American Medical Association recommends calling 1-800-273-8255 for immediate help if you or someone you know is in danger of suicide. See Chapter 15, Crisis Management and Prevention, for more information about suicide, a chart to track your suicidal feelings, and more options.

How can I gauge the severity of my depression and understand how it changes over time?

Following is a checklist to help you evaluate and chart your major depressive symptoms in a form that will help you communicate your condition to your doctor and therapist. Check the boxes that reflect how you have been feeling.

Short Depression Checklist

Check each statement that represents the way you have felt over the last week. Score the questions on a scale of 0 to 5, with 0=not present and 5=very severe.

0 1 2 3 4 5

☐ ☐ ☐ ☐ ☐ ☐ The things I used to enjoy now seem unattractive.

☐ ☐ ☐ ☐ ☐ ☐ I cannot think of any activities I would like to be doing.

☐ ☐ ☐ ☐ ☐ ☐ Even good news cannot stop me from feeling depressed.

☐ ☐ ☐ ☐ ☐ ☐ Food does not seem appealing, and my weight is changing.

☐ ☐ ☐ ☐ ☐ ☐ It takes me a long time to fall asleep after I go to bed.

☐ ☐ ☐ ☐ ☐ ☐ I wake up earlier than I want or need to.

☐ ☐ ☐ ☐ ☐ ☐ I have frequent headaches, stomachaches, or other pains.

☐ ☐ ☐ ☐ ☐ ☐ I feel tired all the time.

☐ ☐ ☐ ☐ ☐ ☐ I constantly worry that I have a serious disease, although there is no proof that I do.

☐ ☐ ☐ ☐ ☐ ☐ My thoughts and actions seem to be in slow motion.

☐ ☐ ☐ ☐ ☐ ☐ I cannot keep negative thoughts from entering my mind.

☐ ☐ ☐ ☐ ☐ ☐ I have thoughts that keep repeating over and over.

☐ ☐ ☐ ☐ ☐ ☐ I have difficulty making decisions that affect my life.

☐ ☐ ☐ ☐ ☐ ☐ I am struggling in work or school.

☐ ☐ ☐ ☐ ☐ ☐ My interest in sex is reduced or gone.

☐ ☐ ☐ ☐ ☐ ☐ I believe I am an undesirable person.

☐ ☐ ☐ ☐ ☐ ☐ I feel hopeless about my future.

☐ ☐ ☐ ☐ ☐ ☐ I think a lot about death.

☐ ☐ ☐ ☐ ☐ ☐ I have been thinking about killing myself.

☐ ☐ ☐ ☐ ☐ ☐ I have made a plan to kill myself.

☐ ☐ ☐ ☐ ☐ ☐ I have set a date to kill myself.

0 1 2 3 4 5

_____ TOTAL SCORE

(Minimum = 0, Maximum = 105)

All this information seems overwhelming—what can I do to fight all these problems?

In the following pages, you will find many simple, practical solutions to help make your depression go away and keep it from coming back. We will cover medication therapy, psychotherapy, healthy lifestyles that decrease your depression, stress-reduction techniques, crisis management, psychotherapy you can do at home, and special tips for depressed women. But first, we need to find out if you have unipolar major depression.

Chapter 3   # DIAGNOSIS AND CAUSES

- Why are there so many different names for depression?
- How is unipolar major depression diagnosed?
- Why can't everyone diagnose their own depression?
- What is the single most important symptom of unipolar major depression?
- My sadness seems reasonable and bearable—how much sadness is normal?
- Why are so many physical symptoms in the definition of depression?
- Are there blood tests or brain scans that diagnose unipolar major depression?
- Can't anyone have these "diagnostic" criteria?
- Is major depression primarily physical or mental?
- How does unipolar major depression start?
- What role does genetics play in depression?
- Do you have to have the genes for depression in order to get depressed?
- What exactly do you mean when you talk about stress?
- What part of the brain is responsible for depression?
- What's the relationship between brain chemicals and depression?
- Does early childhood abuse cause major depression?
- Is "unipolar major depression" just another term for life stress?
- Why do I get depressed without anything stressful happening to me?
- It seems like my depression is caused by my negative thoughts—is that normal?
- How do these negative thoughts affect me?
- Is there a biological reason for depression?

Why are there so many different names for depression?

When most people say "depression," they mean unipolar major depression, which is the subject of this book. Other names for unipolar major depression include clinical depression, major depressive illness, major depression with melancholic features, or simply unipolar depression. These terms all refer to the same illness, located at the same place in the brain and affecting the same brain cells and chemicals. Other diseases that have "depression" in the title (like bipolar depression), or conditions where people feel sad or blue (like cancer, chronic pain, or brain injury) are different from major depression and involve different brain cells and brain chemicals than unipolar major depression.

How is unipolar major depression diagnosed?

Doctors in the United States and many other countries use a manual of diagnostic criteria drawn from a large body of medical research and clinicians' experience. It is published by the American Psychiatric Association, and it is called the *Diagnostic and Statistical Manual of Mental Illness, Fourth Edition*. The criteria are written somewhat technically for doctors (see Appendix B). Here is an easy-to-use checklist that can help you determine if you are clinically depressed.

CRITERIA THAT DOCTORS USE TO DIAGNOSE MAJOR UNIPOLAR DEPRESSION

Check each statement that represents the way you have felt over the last two weeks.

☐ 1. Have you had a feeling of sadness nearly every day?

☐ 2. Have you lost interest or enjoyment in nearly all your activities?

☐ 3. Has your appetite changed OR have you lost more than five pounds without trying to diet?

☐ 4. Have you had difficulty going to sleep OR are you waking too early?

☐ 5. Have your thoughts or behavior slowed so much that other people notice?

☐ 6. Have you had low energy OR been fatigued nearly every day?

☐ 7. Have you had feelings of worthlessness OR guilt?

☐ 8. Have you had difficulty thinking OR concentrating OR making decisions?

☐ 9. Have you been thinking of death or suicide, OR have you planned or tried suicide?

Here's How to Score

Step 1. If you did not check either Question 1 or 2 above, stop—you probably do *not* have unipolar major depression. If you checked Question 1 or 2, go to Step 2.

Step 2. If you checked five or more of Questions 1–9, go to Step 3.

Step 3. If the sum of all these problems is severe enough to interfere with your work, school, family relationships, or social activities, you meet the official criteria for unipolar major depression. Go to a doctor who can evaluate you to determine if you really do have the disorder.

Why can't everyone diagnose their own depression?

It takes a lot of training to learn how to apply these simple criteria perfectly. During their training, psychiatrists spend hours every day for months on end at the hospital, interviewing one volunteer patient after another in the company of a panel of experienced clinicians. After the student doctor makes and explains his or her diagnosis, each of the experienced doctors discusses why that diagnosis was right or wrong. This continues for years until doctors are proficient in the complex art of diagnosis.

It is essential that everyone associated with unipolar major depression know and understand the official diagnostic criteria. Just knowing how unipolar major depression is defined will greatly help you to understand it. However, a definitive diagnosis requires a one-on-one examination by a trained doctor, not just self-evaluation.

What is the single most important symptom of unipolar major depression?

The inability to enjoy activities and experiences that you used to enjoy is at the heart of unipolar major depression. This inability is called *anhedonia* (literally "not enjoying"), and it is the most important of all the questions on the checklist. If you have anhedonia, it does not matter whether your emotions are mainly sad, anxious, angry, or anything else; you still qualify for the diagnosis of unipolar major depression if you have enough of the physical and mental symptoms from the checklist.

My sadness seems reasonable and bearable—how much sadness is normal?

Sadness is normal when it is short and it does not interfere with your life. If sadness persists more than a few weeks, it may signal an underlying problem. If the sadness you feel is strong enough that you have discontinued, changed, or altered your work routine, school performance, family interactions, or social life, then your sadness is probably too much.

Unipolar major depression can easily be distinguished from simple bad moods because depression is accompanied by physical symptoms, mental slowing, poor concentration, and thoughts of death that are usually not present if you're just in a bad mood. If this sounds like you, my advice is to go to a psychiatrist or other doctor and find out for sure.

Why are so many physical symptoms in the definition of depression?

If you take a close look at the diagnostic criteria in Appendix B, you will see that physical problems such as insomnia, fatigue, low energy, physical slowing, and change in appetite are an essential part of major depression. No one can be given the diagnosis of unipolar major depression unless he or she experiences several important physical symptoms. This is one of the keys to understanding that unipolar major depression is a real medical disease like a heart attack, high blood pressure, diabetes, or hepatitis. The physical symptoms illustrate that there are powerful physical and neurological forces at work in unipolar major depression.

Are there blood tests or brain scans that diagnose unipolar major depression?

In internal medicine, drawing blood, spinal taps, radiographic studies, and exploratory surgeries are done because internists and surgeons cannot see into the body to observe disease processes in the liver, lungs, pancreas, kidneys, etc. Unlike these internal disorders, unipolar major depression is a disease that manifests in emotions, physical symptoms, thoughts, and behaviors that *can* be observed directly by both doctor and patient. Your doctor can find out about your internal emotions and thoughts simply by asking you. Right now, sitting in a room and talking to a psychiatrist is the best way of detecting the presence of unipolar major depression, because we can observe the depression in action.

Although scientists are working hard on improving brain scans, they have nothing that can reliably detect unipolar major depression at this time. There are no tests for the reduced serotonin or other neurochemicals involved in depression, because the amounts contained in the gaps between your brain cells are too tiny.

Can't anyone have these "diagnostic" criteria?

It certainly seems like everyone has had bad sleep habits or poor appetite at some time in their lives. However, to be diagnosed with unipolar major depression, sad feelings or loss of interest in life have to be present along with several specific physical and mental symptoms at the same time (see Appendix B). These depressed symptoms must be severe enough that they interfere with your normal work, school, family, and social life. If this sounds like you, you may have unipolar major depression.

Is major depression primarily physical or mental?

Unipolar major depression exists simultaneously on many levels of a person, including physical, emotional, and intellectual. Unraveling the causes of depression is like slicing through a Black Forest cake. The farther down you cut, the more layers you see, yet they are all part of the same cake.

How does unipolar major depression start?

Unipolar major depression originates in genetics and family inheritance. If one of your parents, brothers, or sisters has unipolar major depression, then you have a 20 percent chance of inheriting it yourself. If both of your parents have genes for depression, you have a 50 percent chance of getting it. However, even if no one in your family has unipolar major depression, the depressive genes can occur spontaneously on their own.

For example, imagine there was someone who had a set of genes identical to yours (like an identical twin). No matter whether the two of you were raised in different countries, in different families, or by different parents who were not depressed, if you both had the depression genes, you both would probably be depressed. Studies like these have been done with identical twins who were separated at birth. If both had the depression genes, then both were more often than not depressed, although they had grown up and lived under different conditions.

What role does genetics play in depression?

The genes for depression cause peoples' brains to overreact to stress. When subjected to stress, everyone secretes steroid stress hormones in their bodies and excitatory neurochemicals in their brains. However, the brains of individuals with unipolar major depression do not shut off the secretion of these stress chemicals when the stress is over. When these stress chemicals are present at levels that are too high for too long, they damage and kill cells in the brain, contributing to unipolar major depression.

Moreover, after an episode of unipolar major depression begins, it also provokes the secretion of stress steroid hormones and excitatory neurochemicals. Thus, depression causes a stress reaction that builds on itself.

For example, imagine a high school student who wants to make the winning goal to end her soccer game. Her brain and body release steroid stress hormones and norepinephrine so that she is stronger and quicker and has more endurance. Her body is wired, and her mind is on fire, ready to move. She races down the field and makes the winning goal; then her body quickly turns off the stress response, and she returns to normal again.

Unfortunately, people who have the genes for unipolar major depression cannot turn off their stress response. When they experience stress from jobs, deadlines, family trouble, medical illness, or extreme excitement, large quantities of steroid stress hormones and norepinephrine come pouring into their brains and cannot be stopped. Every day, this stress overload is fatiguing and killing cells in their brains, bringing on unipolar major depression.

Do you have to have the genes for depression in order to get depressed?

We are not sure of that yet. Some people prefer to believe that their depression is a one-time event triggered by an outside tragedy, and it may be. However, it is unlikely that circumstances alone cause unipolar major depression—most people who are exposed to severe circumstances do not become depressed. And often the first depressive episode is followed by others through the years that have either minor triggers or none at all.

What exactly do you mean when you talk about stress?

Stress is medically defined as the process of mental and physical activation in which your body secretes a flood of steroid stress hormones and excitatory chemicals into your body and brain. Stress causes the classic "fight or flight" response that increases your brain activity, makes your heart pound, increases your blood pressure, raises your body temperature, and makes you pant and perspire when something scares or overexcites you. Adrenaline is a well-known example of one of the nervous system chemicals (neurochemicals) that are released when you're under stress.

Stress chemicals are meant to be released only briefly in times of extreme danger or excitement, but if you have unipolar major depression, you cannot turn off this response, and stress chemicals are constantly flooding into your body and brain, damaging brain cells and causing a depressive episode.

In addition, this overactive stress response depletes the brain's natural healing chemicals, including an important one called "brain-derived neurotrophic factor" or BDNF. Individuals with unipolar major depression do not produce enough BDNF to heal the brain cells that have been damaged by stress or to help give birth to new brain cells to replace the ones that have been killed. The lack of BDNF, and the depression it causes, can have serious consequences; studies have shown that depressed individuals who committed suicide had insufficient amounts of BDNF in their brains. Fortunately, antidepressants (as well as exercise and creative activities) can bring BDNF levels back to normal again.

What part of the brain is responsible for depression?

In the brain, the hypothalamus, the pituitary gland, and the adrenal glands are responsible for the control of emotion, behavior, and important brain neurochemicals. When the brain recognizes a stressful situation, a signal is sent to the hypothalamus, which signals the pituitary, which signals the adrenal glands to release stimulating steroids (like cortisol) and excitatory neurochemicals (like norepinephrine). These saturate the areas of the brain that control thought and behavior (frontal lobes), emotions (the amygdala), memory (the hippocampus), and alertness (the brain stem), where they fatigue and damage brain cells. Eventually these damaged brain cells die. The loss of these cells is at the heart of unipolar major depression. You can even see the hippocampus shrinking in MRI images as depression worsens over time.

Fortunately, studies show that antidepressant treatment stops this cell death, while psychotherapy, healthy life changes, and relaxation techniques can reduce your daily stress.

What's the relationship between brain chemicals and depression?

Important brain pathways are made up of chains of brain cells that conduct signals from one to another by releasing neurochemicals (serotonin, norepinephrine, or dopamine). These chains of brain cells carry signals to the target areas of your brain that turn on and off your alertness, anger, anxiety, appetite, energy, irritability, sadness, sleep, thoughts, and the physical workings of your body. If cells in the chain are damaged by depression, then the pathway is interrupted, and the signal never arrives at its destination, causing a disturbance in your emotions, behavior, and body processes. Adding additional serotonin, norepinephrine, and dopamine to the gaps between the cells makes it easier for damaged cells to pass signals down the chain so that the pathway is not interrupted. All antidepressants add serotonin, norepinephrine, or dopamine to the gaps between brain cells.

Does early childhood abuse cause major depression?

Children who have the depressive genes are especially sensitive to early neglect, malnutrition, deprivation, physical harm, and psychological abuse, particularly at the ages when their brains are still developing. Studies show that early childhood stress can turn on depressive genes and make children vulnerable to depression. For example, one study showed that individuals who carried depressive genes were more likely to be depressed as adults if they had been abused as children.

Children in hostile environments also develop maladaptive stress-management habits that often continue into adulthood. For example, strategies like denying the existence of problems, withdrawal, and isolation may help children survive hostile environments, but when these once-useful habits persist in adults, they serve no purpose but to cause psychological problems.

Also, children who inherit genes for depression often have parents with unipolar major depression or depressive tendencies. When parents' depression is severe, it can decrease the effectiveness of their parenting, and stressful family environments are more likely to develop.

Is "unipolar major depression" just another term for life stress?

No. Stressful life events help drive unipolar major depression, but depression is not just stress. The majority of individuals with early child abuse and traumatic adult experiences do not get unipolar major depression. On the other hand, much milder stressors can trigger unipolar major depression in people who have depressive genes. Although stress can help trigger depression, depression is much more than just a stress response.

Why do I get depressed without anything stressful happening to me?

For individuals who have unipolar major depression, an episode can be triggered by internal stressors like anger, fear, fatigue, and natural hormonal changes, or external stressors such as sickness and overwork. You do not have to experience any single big event to trigger a depressive episode; several moderate stressors can add up to a big load of stress. And once an episode of depression starts, it increases the stress reaction in the brain. After you have the first episode of unipolar major depression, others come more easily.

It seems like my depression is caused by my negative thoughts—is that normal?

Psychologists know that thoughts are a very important part of unipolar major depression. As you become depressed, your thoughts are drawn ever closer to negative memories and perceptions. The more you think, the more negative your thoughts become. This negative thinking gradually crowds out positive, happy, and optimistic thoughts until everything you can think of leads to thoughts of unhappiness, pain, and death.

For example, when you're depressed, a chain of thought might go like this: "I have to remember to pay my rent today. If I don't pay my rent, I could get thrown out of my apartment. And if I get thrown out of my apartment, I'll have to live on the street. And if I have to live on the street, my life would be hopeless." In this way, depressive thinking can turn a neutral thought about paying rent into proof that life is hopeless.

Depression causes negative thoughts to come into your mind on their own, apparently out of nowhere. We call these "intrusive thoughts," and when they begin to repeat in your mind, we call them "circular thoughts." For example, a depressed woman suddenly had the thought that her child was sick, although she knew her child was fine. As the day went by, the thought kept repeating in her mind, saying "my child is sick, my child is sick, my child is sick," until she was worn down and weary from the negative thinking.

How do these negative thoughts affect me?

Gradually, living with negative thoughts makes you change your beliefs about yourself and the rest of the world. You come to expect loss and disappointment. Self-criticism becomes a habit. Your mind begins to distort your perceptions of the world around you, so that you filter out good things and only notice things that are dark and horrible. As these changes occur, you feel your life being pulled farther and farther down. In this state, it is easy to trigger your negative emotions, and you find yourself feeling angry or sad or crying at little things. (We will review solutions to these problems in subsequent chapters.)

Behavioral psychologists have observed that depressed individuals withdraw from the activities they used to enjoy and avoid being with the people they used to like. They stop going to places they used to like and eating the foods they liked to eat. Their associations become so negative that even the thought of doing an activity that used to be pleasant makes them feel miserable. Behavioral therapy reverses these behaviors and helps you remember how you acted before you were depressed (see Chapter 9, Seeking Therapy).

Is there a biological reason for depression?

It's likely that depression exists in our human gene pool because in the past it helped keep people alive during life-threatening adversities like natural disasters, famines, plagues, and wars. Emotional paralysis, the inability to make decisions, low motivation, decreased energy, and decreased hunger would have helped depressed individuals isolate and stay inside until disaster passed. Lowered metabolism and activity would have helped depressed individuals live longer without food or shelter. Childhood depression would have helped children stay alive through epidemics and widespread child abuse by forcing them to keep a low profile and avoid contact with others until they were old enough to take care of themselves. Depressed individuals were the survivors.

Chapter 4

SIMILAR AND COEXISTING DISORDERS

- Are there other conditions that can get confused with unipolar major depression?
- What's the difference between major depression and bipolar disorder?
- What is dysthymia?
- What is borderline personality disorder?
- How does the depression that follows a brain injury differ from unipolar major depression?
- Could my chronic medical condition be causing symptoms of depression?
- What is the most common medical cause of depressive symptoms?
- Could a medication I'm taking make me feel depressed?
- Could my sleep apnea be causing my depressed symptoms?
- Are thyroid deficiency and depression related?
- Does low testosterone cause the same symptoms as depression?
- What can I do about my depression?

Are there other conditions that can get confused with unipolar major depression?

Despite wider public recognition of major depression and its treatment, misdiagnosis is still a problem. Unless doctors strictly adhere to the official diagnostic criteria (see Appendix B), depression can be confused with other, unrelated illnesses that have some overlapping symptoms. This can cause a patient to get incorrect treatment that may be ineffective or even dangerous.

What's the difference between major depression and bipolar disorder?

Bipolar depression and unipolar major depression are frequently confused, though they are totally different diseases. Bipolar depression has different symptoms that originate in different locations in the brain and involve different types of brain neurochemicals, and it is treated with different types of medications and therapy. In general, patients with bipolar depression tend to sleep too much and eat too much, and their sadness can easily be relieved by happy events, if only for a few hours or days. Although they experience intrusive thoughts, patients with bipolar depression usually do not obsess on death like those suffering from unipolar major depression. In addition, patients with bipolar depression experience anxiety, agitation, edginess, distractibility, and isolation, and they are more likely to take unnecessary risks like driving while intoxicated or having unprotected sex. In the doctor's office, patients with bipolar depression are more likely to look expansive, anxious, and angry, compared to the sad, quiet, withdrawn demeanor typical of unipolar major depression.

If antidepressants are mistakenly given to people with bipolar depression, they may trigger worse depression, suicidal tendencies, mania, or psychosis, and they may cause bipolar disorder to become irreversibly worse.

What is dysthymia?

Dysthymia resembles unipolar major depression, but with important differences. In dysthymia, people experience sad, negative emotions almost every hour of every day all their lives. The definition of dysthymia also requires two of the following: poor appetite or overeating, insomnia or oversleeping, fatigue, poor concentration, feelings of hopelessness, or low self-esteem. Most doctors agree that dysthymia does not respond well to antidepressants or psychotherapy targeted for unipolar major depression.

What is borderline personality disorder?

Borderline personality disorder is a lifelong condition of unstable emotions and relationships. Individuals suffering from borderline personality disorder experience brief, rapid mood swings into intense anger, rage, sadness, or anxiety. Borderline personality disorder is also associated with impulsive acts of self-mutilation and multiple suicide attempts. In addition, individuals with borderline personality disorder usually feel severe emotional numbness and emptiness, and they may overreact to perceived abandonment. Neuropsychological testing shows cognitive deficits in borderline patients that increase with the severity of their illness.

Antidepressants are unlikely to work well for borderline personality disorder. Psychodynamic psychotherapy, structured group psychotherapy, and supportive psychotherapy are sometimes helpful.

How does the depression that follows a brain injury differ from unipolar major depression?

Organic depression is a distinct type of depression that comes with apathy, low motivation, increased anger, and impulsive behavior; it usually develops after a brain injury that causes loss of consciousness. Accidents, infections, poisoning, strokes, and trauma can all injure the brain, disrupting brain pathways and disturbing emotions and thoughts. For example, football players who have had previous brain concussions are three times more likely to be given a diagnosis of depression than other people.

Nevertheless, brain injury is different from unipolar major depression and needs different treatment. Sometimes brain injury responds to psychotherapy and small doses of antidepressants or medicines used to treat epileptic seizures.

Could my chronic medical condition be causing symptoms of depression?

Quite possibly. Many medical conditions create slow, dulled thinking, negative emotions, or other symptoms similar to those of unipolar major depression. However, most of the diseases that cause depressive symptoms (like strokes, heart failure, diabetes, etc.) can be detected by the history, examination, and laboratory tests that you get in a good physical examination from your internist or family doctor. This is why it is a good idea to have a physical examination before beginning depression treatment.

Following is a list of such medical problems that can confuse or complicate the diagnosis and treatment of unipolar major depression.

Alcoholism	Diabetes
Alzheimer's Disease	Drug Abuse
Anemia (from B-vitamin or iron deficiency)	Heart Failure
	HIV Infection
Asthma	Huntington's Disease
Cancer	Kidney Disease
Chronic Obstructive Pulmonary Disorder (COPD)	Menopause
	Multiple Sclerosis

Myasthenia Gravis
Parkinson's Disease
Perimenopause
Premenstrual Syndrome
Rheumatoid Arthritis
Sleep Apnea

Stroke
Systemic Lupus Erythematosis
Temporal Lobe Epilepsy
Thyroid Disorder
Viral Hepatitis

What is the most common medical cause of depressive symptoms?

Alcohol and drug abuse are by far the most common causes of depressive symptoms. Sometimes it is impossible to tell the difference between unipolar major depression and substance abuse, and doctors may not know whether they are treating one or the other. Alcohol and drug abuse causes brain injuries similar to the brain cell damage caused by unipolar major depression. Substance abuse can also make existing unipolar major depression worse.

If you feel depressed, give yourself a one-month trial off alcohol and drugs. If you cannot do that, start with a two-week trial abstinence. If you feel a lot better after a few weeks, you will probably want to continue your sobriety. Alcoholics Anonymous and other twelve-step programs are usually good treatment for alcoholism and drug abuse.

Could a medication I'm taking make me feel depressed?

Several medications can produce depressive symptoms. Stay away from prescribed steroids like prednisone and the anabolic steroids used by bodybuilders. A few medications for heart problems like Serpasi (reserpine), antivirals like Foscavir (foscarnet), and oral acne medicines like Accutane (isotretinoin) can trigger or aggravate unipolar major depression. Ask your primary care doctor to make sure you do not get any medications that can cause or increase depression.

Could my sleep apnea be causing my depressed symptoms?

If you have trouble breathing at night, you may be absorbing too much carbon dioxide in your blood, leading to mental slowing and foggy thinking. Sleep apnea is also associated with heart problems, so get this problem treated if your doctor recommends it.

Are thyroid deficiency and depression related?

Thyroid deficiency alone can cause some depressive symptoms. Together with unipolar major depression, thyroid deficiency can make depressive symptoms worse and make major depression harder to treat. If you feel slowed down or exhibit symptoms of depression, you should ask your doctor for a thyroid test if you have not had one within six months. Three laboratory tests for thyroid function many psychiatrists use are TSH, serum Free-T4 and serum Free-T3.

Does low testosterone cause the same symptoms as depression?

Sex hormone diseases are often confused with unipolar major depression—one study showed that men with testicular diseases were four times more likely to be diagnosed with depression.

Testosterone levels decline naturally in all men after forty years of age, but few of them develop unipolar major depression. Also, testosterone has been prescribed as a treatment for depression with little success. (Testosterone supplementation has improved the mood of some patients with *bipolar* depression, however, and also thrown some of them into mania.)

If you are concerned about your testosterone level, ask your doctor about it during your next physical examination. There is a blood test for measuring testosterone levels.

What can I do about my depression?

Treating and eliminating the symptoms of depression is one of the most rewarding, upbeat, and exciting things you'll ever do for yourself. As you begin your treatment, you will gain more control over your thoughts and emotions, and you will move closer to your most natural self. You will find the strength to enjoy the activities you used to enjoy and to rediscover the support of family and friends. You will think more clearly, solve problems more easily, and begin to undo problems that developed during your depression episode. You will have the wonderful feeling of lifting your emotions from the black pit of depression. We'll start to examine the solutions for depression in the next chapter.

Chapter 5

NEWER ANTIDEPRESSANT MEDICATIONS

- How do antidepressants work?
- Do antidepressants actually heal and replace damaged brain cells?
- Will antidepressants help *anyone* who is sad or depressed feel better?
- Will depression just go away on its own if I wait long enough?
- Are there any antidepressants that have no side effects?
- Do antidepressant drugs build up in your system over the years until your body is full of toxins?
- Do antidepressants cause suicide?
- Are antidepressants just a crutch?
- What predicts a good response to antidepressants?
- Why are some antidepressants called SSRIs?
- Is Celexa a good antidepressant?
- Is Cymbalta a new antidepressant that works in a special way?
- Is Desyrel an old medication?
- Is Effexor any better than other antidepressants?
- What is Lexapro like?
- Is Luvox often prescribed?
- What are the benefits and drawbacks of Paxil?
- Why is Prozac the most recognized antidepressant?
- Does Remeron have bad side effects?
- Whatever happened to Serzone?
- What are the advantages of Wellbutrin?
- Will Zoloft make me sleepy at work?
- What is serotonin syndrome?
- What should I be aware of when taking antidepressants?

How do antidepressants work?

Antidepressants help your body heal brain cells and replace natural brain chemicals that have been affected by depression. Depressed individuals have an overactive stress response that damages and kills cells in their brains. When brain cells are damaged, they cannot carry the signals that control emotions, thoughts, concentration, appetite, energy, sleep, and behavior. Antidepressants correct this problem in two ways. First, antidepressants get your body to produce more of its natural brain-healing chemicals. By increasing the amount of these brain-healing factors, antidepressants help repair damaged brain cells and help protect your brain from being damaged in the future so your depression will not return.

Second, antidepressants help the brain to secrete more natural brain neurochemicals in the gaps between brain cells so damaged brain cells can fire more easily and work more normally. As a result, signals controlling mood, thoughts, and behavior can travel through the brain without interruption.

Do antidepressants actually heal and replace damaged brain cells?

Most antidepressants are thought to stimulate the production of natural healing and protective biochemicals, including brain-derived neurotrophic factor (BDNF), nerve growth factor (NGF), and neurotrophin-3 (NT-3). The ability of antidepressants to heal the brain is not yet fully appreciated. We may find that antidepressants also have a role in repairing brain cells damaged by injury, disease, toxins, and abused drugs, or in helping to slow down the aging process.

Will antidepressants help *anyone* who is sad or depressed feel better?

Antidepressants only help individuals with unipolar major

depression. For example, if we pick an average person walking down the sidewalk in front of my office and give him an antidepressant, he will not feel any happier. Antidepressants work by healing brain damage. They are not "happy pills."

Will depression just go away on its own if I wait long enough?

Depressive episodes *usually* go away within six to twelve months, although some depressive episodes last longer, and some never go away. The longer the episode lasts, the more of your brain cells are damaged and killed. Even if the episode goes away on its own, six to twelve months is plenty of time to be fired from your job, lose your house, alienate your friends and family, suffer accidents and injuries, and do and say other things that can have a horrible impact on your life. If the episode lasts too long unchecked, you may pile up bills from doctors' visits and hospital stays that you will be paying back for years. If you suspect you have unipolar major depression, it's important to seek help before the symptoms of the disease start to affect your future.

Are there any antidepressants that have no side effects?

No antidepressant has a side-effect profile that's ideal for everyone—however, side effects are not the reason you are taking an antidepressant. Every antidepressant has different effects, and the most important issue is whether the antidepressant will be effective at stopping your depression. You do not want to end up taking a medication with no side effects that does not stop your depression symptoms. If there are side effects, these usually occur within the first month or so after beginning or increasing the medication and tend to disappear over days to weeks.

Do antidepressant drugs build up in your system over the years until your body is full of toxins?

This old wives' tale is probably being spread by people who want to defraud you of your money by offering "cures" for "built-up antidepressant poisons." People have been taking antidepressants for more than fifty years. We have plenty of experience with our current antidepressants, and none of them produces any poisons—antidepressants simply get your brain to produce more of the natural neurochemicals that help it to function normally. You do not need to waste your money on buying products or paying anyone to "detoxify" your body from antidepressants, because they do not produce any toxins.

Most antidepressants are gone from the body in a few days (see tables on pages 47 and 69), and many are gone from the body in less than twenty-four hours. This is why most antidepressants are taken daily. A few antidepressants stay around longer, and the amount in your body initially increases with more doses but levels off over a matter of days or weeks.

Once people find an antidepressant dose that relieves their symptoms, they can usually take the same dose for a lifetime without suffering any problems or needing a change in dose.

Do antidepressants cause suicide?

The use of antidepressants to treat depression has saved hundreds of thousands of lives from suicides, accidents, and poor self-care. For example, research has shown that Prozac alone saves about 2,400 lives a year from suicide. That adds up to over fifty thousand lives saved since its introduction.

When you hear stories about antidepressants failing to work or causing unexpected problems, recognize that most of these stories involve people who are misdiagnosed. Antidepressants are not sold, licensed, or intended to treat grief, bipolar depression, dysthymia, brain injury, personality disorders, heart disease, hormonal imbalance, diabetes, etc., nor are they meant to treat people with no diagnosis who feel sad. The effects are unpredictable when antidepressants are given against directions to someone who does not have unipolar major depression. For example, mistakenly giving someone with bipolar disorder an antidepressant may trigger a manic, depressed, or psychotic episode that could culminate in suicide or violence. But if you are accurately diagnosed with unipolar major depression, appropriate antidepressants will help you, not hurt you.

Are antidepressants just a crutch?

Antidepressants are a tool, not a crutch. I would never hammer a nail with my hand so I could be sure I was "doing it on my own." In addition to making you feel better quickly, antidepressants can restore your concentration, memory, and logical thinking skills. If you choose to take an antidepressant, you will be able to think more clearly and progress further and faster in your recovery.

What predicts a good response to antidepressants?

Discussing treatment options and potential benefits and risks thoroughly with your doctor and making decisions together is the best way of improving success in treating unipolar major depression. You should work in close partnership with your doctor and discuss different forms of treatment until you find the one that will work best for you.

Scientifically, the only predictor of future success with an antidepressant is past performance. If a medication has worked well for you in the past, it is just good common sense to go with a winning treatment. Similarly, if you have a relative with symptoms like yours and they are taking an antidepressant that works well, then you should consider taking this medication.

Why are some antidepressants called SSRIs?

SSRI stands for *selective serotonin reuptake inhibitor*, which is just another name for modern antidepressants that help the body release more serotonin into the gaps between brain cells. Antidepressants that help the body release serotonin *and* norepinephrine are called SNRIs, which stands for *serotonin and norepinephrine reuptake inhibitors*. Some authorities are using the term DRIs for *double reuptake inhibitors* and TRIs for *triple reuptake inhibitors* to describe antidepressants that stimulate the release of two or three of the neurochemicals serotonin, norepinephrine, and dopamine. Because they act differently, antidepressants all feel different and are more effective for some individuals than others.

In general, serotonin decreases depression, anxiety, aggression, and sleep, while increasing appetite and weight gain. Serotonin antidepressants usually prolong the time to reach orgasm. Most modern antidepressants have a strong serotonin effect.

Norepinephrine generally increases physical energy, motivation, and anxiety, while decreasing appetite, weight, and sleep.

Dopamine tends to increase alertness, concentration, and optimism, while decreasing appetite.

You can see the relative amounts of serotonin, norepinephrine, and dopamine that each antidepressant stimulates in the tables on pages 47 and 69. (The information in these tables came from an international public database of scientific binding studies, the NIMH-PDSP database organized by Prof. B. Roth; see Appendix A, Resources.)

Characteristics of Important Modern Antidepressants[1]
SSRIs, SNRIs, and Others

Name	Generic	Serotonin	Norepinephrine	Dopamine	Time to Leave the Body[2]
Celexa	citalopram	+++			4½ days
Cymbalta	duloxetine	++++	+++	+	1½ days
Desyrel	trazodone	+			1 day
Effexor	venlafaxine	++	++		1½ days[3]
Lexapro	escitalopram	+++			4 days
Luvox	fluvoxamine	+++	+		2 days
Paxil	paroxetine	++++	++	+	2½ days[3]
Prozac	fluoxetine	+++	+		5 weeks
Remeron	mirtazapine	+	+		4 days
Wellbutrin	buproprion		+	+	2½ days[3]
Zoloft	sertraline	++++	+	++	8 days

[1] The amount of serotonin, norepinephrine, and dopamine refers to the strength of the binding to the transporter protein that is responsible for increasing serotonin, norepinephrine, and dopamine in the gaps between brain cells in a chain. These values are based on data drawn from the NIMH-PDSP database and reflect a K_i range of 0–1,000 (see Appendix A, Resources).

[2] This is the amount of time it takes for 87.5 percent of the original antidepressant, and/or its metabolites to leave the body. This comes from multiplying the published time it takes for one-half of the medication to leave the body times three.

[3] This time applies to the original, regular-release pills: controlled-release or time-release formulations may be different.

Is Celexa a good antidepressant?

Celexa (generic name: citalopram) is an SSRI antidepressant that helps the brain strongly increase serotonin but not norepinephrine or dopamine. Celexa reaches its peak level quickly, about four hours after you take it. Nevertheless, Celexa stays around a long time; it takes about four and a half days to leave your body. This means that after taking Celexa for a week, it can reach a blood level of about two and a half times your original dose.

Celexa has several side effects, but none pose a danger to your overall health. Patients have reported fatigue, sleepiness, insomnia, increased perspiration, migraine headaches, missed menstrual periods, delayed ejaculation, and impotence. As is the case with all antidepressants, most of these side effects decrease or go away in days to weeks as your body adjusts to the medication.

Celexa comes in 10-, 20-, and 40-milligram generic tablets and a peppermint-flavored oral solution containing 10 milligrams per teaspoon. It is usually started at 20 milligrams per day and increased to 40 milligrams per day. Elders clear Celexa from their bodies more slowly than younger people, and they may need one-half the usual dose.

Unfortunately, Celexa seems to have few remarkable features. Many patients are lukewarm about it, and it can seem as though it doesn't remove all their depressive symptoms.

Is Cymbalta a new antidepressant that works in a special way?

Cymbalta (generic name: duloxetine) is an antidepressant that helps the body increase serotonin at low doses, norepinephrine at moderate doses, and dopamine only at higher doses, as the table shows. Cymbalta is called an SNRI, which stands for "serotonin and norepinephrine reuptake inhibitor." Right now, because there is only one other modern antidepressant calling itself an SNRI (the other is Effexor), it makes Cymbalta seem special. However, when you read about the older tricyclic antidepressants and MAOIs, you will realize there are many antidepressants that increase both serotonin and norepinephrine.

In addition to its use in depression, Eli Lilly and Company promotes Cymbalta for the treatment of chronic pain such as fibromyalgia and the nerve pain that accompanies diabetes. Because it increases norepinephrine, Cymbalta works better for this pain than the mainly serotonin antidepressants like Celexa or Lexapro. It is sometimes used as a preventative treatment for migraine headaches. Low doses of older, cheaper, norepinephrine-stimulating tricyclic antidepressants (such as Norpramin and Pamelor) can also reduce the pain of diabetes or migraine; chronic pain in the neck, shoulders, and lower back; and foot pain caused by nerve damage or alcoholism, although they are not specifically licensed for this use.

Cymbalta's side-effect profile resembles some of the older tricyclic antidepressants. At sixty milligrams per day, patients report nausea, sleepiness, constipation, and dry mouth. In one study, nausea was the most common reason patients gave for wanting to stop their Cymbalta. There is little evidence that Cymbalta causes weight gain. Perhaps the nausea caused by Cymbalta makes food seem less attractive. Cymbalta is also associated with sexual side effects including decreased interest in sex and delayed time to orgasm.

Cymbalta is available in 20-, 30-, and 60-milligram tablets. The usual dose is 40 to 60 milligrams per day, and there is little to be gained by increasing the dose over 60 milligrams per day. After you stop taking it, Cymbalta stays in your body for one and a half days.

Carefully discuss a prescription for Cymbalta with your doctor. There are other antidepressants that increase serotonin and norepinephrine just as well, are cheaper, and have less annoying side effects.

Is Desyrel an old medication?

Desyrel (generic name: trazodone) can be a wonderful antidepressant, although it's mostly ignored. Research studies show that Desyrel is as effective against depression as any traditional antidepressant. Desyrel was developed in Italy in the 1960s, and it is in use all over the world. It is one of the antidepressants that helps the body release more serotonin but has little effect on norepinephrine or dopamine.

Desyrel has a so-called heterocyclic structure, which puts it in its own class, different from SSRIs, SNRIs, tricyclics, or any other antidepressant. Desyrel can be combined with many other antidepressants to increase the amount of serotonin that is released into the brain.

Desyrel can also help you sleep at night, and it can even improve the quality of your sleep by normalizing the amount of time you spend in restorative dreaming and deep sleep. This can help you get better rest from the same number of sleep hours. Most people fall asleep within about twenty minutes after taking their Desyrel.

Desyrel works by a different mechanism than the usual sedative sleeping pills, and it can help you get to sleep and stay asleep without becoming addicted. However, it is not licensed for this use. In addition, you will need to work with your doctor to find the right dose for you. If you take too little, you will not fall asleep, and if you take too much, it will be present in your bloodstream when you wake up, and you will feel sleepy.

So what keeps Desyrel from being the world's most popular antidepressant? Well, Desyrel has been around for such a long time that it has long lost its aura of newness and modernity. Desyrel's patent has expired; its generic form is quite inexpensive, and so you will never see any flashy Desyrel promotions on television or the Internet.

You'll likely start at a low dose of 25 milligrams at bedtime and increase the dose over the course of days to weeks—until the Desyrel puts you to sleep at night without leaving you sleepy during the day. This is usually the best starting dose for treating depression. You may end up taking 50 to 100 milligrams at night, although a few patients do better on higher doses up to 300 milligrams.

Patients say that Desyrel takes away their saddest, most negative thoughts and keeps them from overthinking and making mountains out of molehills. Some patients report a slight dulling of emotion. Desyrel is also useful in reducing anxiety, irritability, and anger. You can still get angry while taking Desyrel if you want to, but anger does not flare up as easily.

Patients generally do not experience the typical side effects of tricyclic antidepressants (constipation, dry eyes, etc.) or the typical side effects of SSRI antidepressants (anxiety, edginess, insomnia, or impotence). My patients complain of brief nausea immediately after taking it, but because Desyrel is taken at night, you will probably be asleep and not notice. Some patients have complained of dry mouth or chest congestion in the first few days after starting Desyrel.

Very infrequently, Desyrel can cause a man to have an unusually enlarged penis. This seems to be caused by an exaggeration of the normal process of arousal and erection. Although I have never seen it, textbooks claim that in extreme cases, a few patients' erections swell out of control. If the penis will not go down, you would need to go straight to the emergency room to get an injection that will deflate it and prevent any damage. Although this is a colorful story, it is estimated that this effect occurs in less than 0.002 percent of cases. On hearing this story, some men were anxious to try Desyrel in hopes of getting some increase, but they were all disappointed.

Desyrel comes in 50-, 100-, 150-, and 300-milligram generic tablets. It reaches a peak in your body about one hour after you swallow it, and it is mostly gone from your body in about a day. Clearance may be slower in elders and overweight patients, so these individuals may need smaller doses.

Desyrel can be very helpful for treating unipolar major depression as well as the insomnia, anxiety, and irritability that often accompany it.

Is Effexor any better than other antidepressants?

Effexor (generic name: venlafaxine) helps the brain increase both serotonin and norepinephrine and is classified as a serotonin and norepinephrine reuptake inhibitor (SNRI). The effects of combined serotonin and norepinephrine resemble many of the older tricyclic antidepressants that are quite effective. In Effexor, the norepinephrine effect is greatest at higher doses.

Effexor feels transparent as an antidepressant, so that when it is working well, you may forget you are taking it altogether. Patients say Effexor increases their ability to have positive thoughts, decreases hopelessness, and increases optimism. There is some lifting of the veil of negative thinking. Some headache specialists use daily doses of Effexor to block the recurrence of migraines.

Some studies paint a bad side-effect picture of Effexor, but patients are usually quite satisfied with it. The most common side effects are nausea, sleepiness, dry mouth, and delayed ejaculation in men. It is rare for patients to have any lasting problems with Effexor, particularly if they are prescribed doses less than 150 milligrams. Using the sustained-release form of the drug may further decrease side effects. For the most part, Effexor does not cause weight gain, and it sometimes causes a modest weight loss. Physicians once worried that Effexor might increase blood pressure, but subsequent studies have shown that this is not a clinical concern at moderate doses.

Effexor comes in 25-, 37.5-, 50-, 75-, and 100-milligram regular-release generic tablets and in 37.5-, 75-, and 150-milligram extended-release capsules. The availability of all these different sizes helps your doctor fine-tune your dose to get the best effect.

The usual dose patients find themselves comfortable at is between 75 and 225 milligrams per day. Elders usually take the same doses as other adults. After stopping Effexor, the entire drug and its by-products are mostly gone from your body in just one and a half days.

Pristiq (desvenlafaxine) is a variation on once-daily Effexor that comes in 50- and 100-milligram tablets. I have not seen any particular advantage of this "new" medication to make it preferable to Effexor. I suspect Pristiq was introduced to generate income for the pharmaceutical company now that Effexor's patent has expired.

Effexor is a good alternative to other modern antidepressants. Because Effexor increases norepinephrine at higher doses, it can be added to antidepressants that increase serotonin (like Zoloft) as a double-barreled strategy to squelch lingering symptoms of depression.

What is Lexapro like?

Lexapro (generic name: escitalopram) is an SSRI that helps the body increase serotonin strongly with little effect on norepinephrine or dopamine. Lexapro is a long-lasting variation of Celexa (citalopram) that was promoted by drug companies after the patent on Celexa ran out.

Lexapro is a fairly good antidepressant, and patients have few complaints about it. The most frequent side effects are migraine headaches, weight gain, nausea, insomnia, increased perspiration, fatigue, menstrual cramps, decreased sex drive, difficulty having an orgasm, and delayed ejaculation in men.

Lexapro is given once daily, and it takes about a week for the level to stabilize in the blood after starting the antidepressant. It takes almost four days for one dose of Lexapro to leave the body. This means that the medication tends to accumulate slightly, causing levels in the blood that are higher than expected from the daily dose.

The usual dose of Lexapro is one 10-milligram tablet daily. Lexapro comes in 5-, 10-, and 20-milligram tablets; some studies show no greater benefit with doses over 10 milligrams. Lexapro is also available in a peppermint-flavored liquid solution containing 5 milligrams per teaspoon. Elders clear Lexapro slowly, and they should receive about one-half the usual adult dose.

In general, there seems to be nothing particularly special or awful about Lexapro. It's likely to be helpful, but it might not give you the greatest possible relief of your depression.

Is Luvox often prescribed?

Luvox (generic name: fluvoxamine) works by helping the body increase serotonin at lower doses and norepinephrine at higher doses. Unfortunately for the popularity of Luvox, it was claimed that one of the teenagers involved in a high-school shooting incident was taking it. Subsequently, Luvox was withdrawn from the market (though eventually reintroduced). However, it is not known for certain that the teenager involved had a correct diagnosis of unipolar major depression—the drug could be unfairly maligned because it was used to treat a disease it's not meant for.

Luvox helps stop a patient's repetitive thoughts, slightly dulling sadness and other negative emotions. Patients also say that Luvox makes them sleepy, although daytime sleepiness is decreased by taking Luvox at night. Clinical studies show that at least 10 percent of people taking Luvox complain of dry mouth, stomachache, nervousness, or insomnia. Other side effects include increased perspiration and delayed ejaculation in men.

Luvox takes about five hours to get into the bloodstream after it is ingested. It stays in the body about two days, and it takes about a week to reach a steady concentration in the bloodstream. It comes in 25-, 50-, and 100-milligram generic tablets and 100- and 150-milligram once-daily capsules. Usually Luvox is started at 50 milligrams and increased to 100–300 milligrams taken at bedtime. Caffeine may increase the Luvox level in the blood, whereas smoking can reduce its level. Luvox takes longer to clear in elders and individuals with liver disease, and they should receive lower doses.

Luvox is an effective antidepressant with a number of side effects and no remarkable benefits. It's often a very effective treatment for obsessive-compulsive disorder (OCD) and compulsive habits such as hair-pulling (trichotillomania).

What are the benefits and drawbacks of Paxil?

Paxil (generic name: paroxetine) is an SSRI that appeared on the market early, just after Zoloft and Prozac. Like most antidepressants, Paxil stimulates brain-derived neurotrophic factor (BDNF), which helps heal damaged brain cells and grow new ones. Studies show that Paxil helps the body increase serotonin at lower doses, norepinephrine at moderate doses, and dopamine only at high doses. Patients typically get very good results with Paxil.

Sadness and anxiety generally respond quickly to this medication, and patients report increased ability to continue with their social and work activities. A reduction in irritability, anger, and obsessive thinking usually occurs within several weeks. The most frequent positive effect patients report is a decreased sensitivity to personal stress in relationships and in the work environment. In plain words, their feelings don't get hurt so easily. At the same time, they say that their internal thoughts and feelings seem more bearable and less likely to trigger sad and painful reactions. Paxil is extremely effective for the treatment of social phobia and social anxiety disorder. Paxil can be a doctor's standby remedy for individuals who have tried other SSRIs without getting relief; it can be a wonderfully effective antidepressant.

There is some controversy over whether Paxil makes adolescents and children more likely to become suicidal. Paxil is usually slightly sedating, although it can also be slightly activating in some people. If you find it activating, take your Paxil in the morning; otherwise, take it before you go to bed. There is a definite weight problem associated with Paxil, but it happens gradually. Most of my patients remain thin by making healthy lifestyle choices, limiting calories, avoiding high fat and starchy meals, and exercising.

Mild constipation is a common side effect of Paxil. In clinical trials, over 10 percent of patients taking Paxil reported constipation. Generally, constipation mostly poses a problem for people with prior constipation problems, and it is usually resolved by consuming more vegetables, fruits, and juices.

A few patients have reported muscle tightness in their legs, especially in the first day or two after starting Paxil. This feeling is similar to the physical effect of drinking too many cups of coffee, without the sense of mental activation. This muscle tightness usually goes away after brief stretching or just a conscious effort to relax.

Many people find that their sex drive returns when their depression ebbs after taking Paxil. In most people, Paxil increases the time it takes to have an orgasm during sex. This may be a small effect, and it may be unnoticed. When people feel they climax too quickly during sex, Paxil may normalize their sexual function, and Paxil may actually cure problems of premature ejaculation in men. In other people, it seems to take forever to orgasm, and this is a big problem. Sometimes the sexual side effects go away with time, and if the drug is working well on a person's depression, couples can likely find a way to cure the problem between themselves. Apparently, the more often that someone is able to have an orgasm, the easier it is to have the next one.

Paxil takes about five hours to peak in the bloodstream and about ten days to reach a consistent level. After stopping Paxil, it is gone from the body in about two days. It is available in 10-, 20-, 30-, and 40-milligram generic tablets. Paxil CR, the controlled-release form, comes in 12.5-, 25-, and 37.5-milligram tablets. There does not seem to be much difference between regular and controlled-release tablets (aside from the fact that GlaxoSmithKline charges more for name-brand CR). Patients usually start with 20 milligrams, and dosage is seldom raised. Consequently, there is no need to wait as the dose is slowly increased, and patients do not need to purchase different-sized pills.

Why is Prozac the most recognized antidepressant?

Prozac (generic name: fluoxetine) was one of the first new antidepressants classified as an SSRI, and it is still popular. Prozac helps the body increase serotonin at low doses and norepinephrine at higher doses. Research has also demonstrated that, like most antidepressants, Prozac helps the brain produce more of the natural neurochemicals that heal brain cells and help new ones grow in damaged brain areas. Prozac has been used and studied extensively, and we understand it well. Over 23 million prescriptions for generic fluoxetine were filled in the United States last year.

Patients say that Prozac lowers the overall level of all their emotions, while highly charged negative emotions like strong sadness and anger move into the background. People are aware that negative emotions are present, but they do not break into conscious thought and are easy to ignore.

For some people, the dampening of emotions makes them feel numb or empty. People who are used to feeling strong emotions may miss them and the degree of mental excitement that goes along with them. On the other hand, people who find strong emotions intrusive may be quite satisfied with Prozac.

Many patients experience a slight feeling of activation with Prozac. This serves to counter symptoms of low energy caused by unipolar major depression. This activation also makes many people anxious and makes it harder for them to get to sleep. Clinical studies show that more than 15 percent of those taking Prozac experience anxiety, nervousness, and sleeplessness. Some physicians automatically prescribe antianxiety or sleeping medications for patients who are starting Prozac.

Unfortunately, Prozac has plenty of other side effects, no matter what you might have heard. At least 10 percent of Prozac users report nausea, diarrhea, dry mouth, dizziness, and tremors. It is not a good medication to take if there is any danger of bipolar disorder. Prozac, more often than not, causes mania in people with bipolar disorder.

Sexual side effects make great press, and there is now widespread knowledge that Prozac can alter the sexual response. In addition to the standard SSRI effect of delaying the time to orgasm, patients say they've experienced decreased sensation or numbness in the penis or vagina. Many people have discontinued taking Prozac because of sexual problems.

Prozac takes about seven hours to enter the bloodstream completely, and levels slowly rise until they plateau after about five weeks of treatment. Once in the bloodstream, active Prozac molecules break down into the chemical norfluoxetine, which stays in the body for three to six *weeks*. Prozac and its metabolite stay in the body even longer in elders or patients with liver or kidney problems. All this makes working with Prozac difficult, because it never seems to go away. Prozac is a good antidepressant, but there are better ones available with fewer problems.

Prozac comes in 10-, 20-, and 40-milligram generic tablets and capsules and a mint-flavored liquid containing 20 milligrams per teaspoon. A 20-milligram dose is usually more than enough, and even that may be a large dose for some people.

Does Remeron have bad side effects?

Studies of Remeron (generic name: mirtazapine) show that it helps the body increase serotonin and norepinephrine at the junction of brain cells. Remeron's side effects include significant drowsiness (36 percent), dizziness, increased appetite, and weight gain. Some patients have complained of nightmares after taking Remeron. There are reports of rare (estimated 0.1 percent) cases of lowered white blood cell count while taking Remeron that went away when Remeron was stopped. Many patients do not enjoy taking Remeron.

Some doctors swear by Remeron and use the sedation it causes to help their depressed patients sleep (some patients complain of sleepiness the next day). However, if you need help sleeping, Desyrel can make you sleepy at bedtime with little daytime sleepiness at the right dose, and it is in such common use that we know much about its safety.

Remeron is available in 15-, 30-, and 45-milligram generic tablets. After you stop taking it, Remeron takes about four days to leave your body. Also, Remeron is particularly effective at blocking nausea and vomiting. Some veterinarians reportedly use it to stop dogs from vomiting and to help them gain weight.

Whatever happened to Serzone?

Serzone (generic name: nefazodone) has a weak reuptake effect on both serotonin and norepinephrine. Because it can potentially cause liver damage, it was discontinued by Bristol-Myers Squibb on May 20, 2004, although generic supplies are still available on the Internet. If you find Serzone available in this or any other country, please avoid it.

What are the advantages of Wellbutrin?

Wellbutrin (generic name: buproprion) is unusual among antidepressants because it helps the brain increase the neurochemical dopamine in the gap between brain cells (it increases norepinephrine as well). It is a good antidepressant to try if a patient has already tried a serotonin antidepressant with unsatisfactory results.

Wellbutrin has a stimulating, upbeat effect. Patients tend to like it; they say it increases the number of positive, optimistic thoughts and helps keep their negative emotions in check. In your first few months on Wellbutrin, you should not take it close to bedtime, because it may make it harder to get to sleep. This effect diminishes over time for most people. Wellbutrin does not cause weight gain, and many patients have lost weight while taking Wellbutrin. It does not cause sexual problems; in fact, several doctors have tried giving Wellbutrin to improve sexual function in their depressed patients, but without much success. (Wellbutrin has increased sex drive in patients with bipolar depression, as it drove them closer to mania.)

The norepinephrine effects of Wellbutrin may be helpful to some patients who suffer from asthma.

Wellbutrin's main side effects are insomnia, weight loss, and slight nausea right after taking the pill. This nausea usually goes away in a few days to weeks. If nausea is a problem at first, you can relieve it by eating something small at the same time that you take the medicine. Half a cracker is usually enough.

Because of Wellbutrin's activating effect, it has sometimes been tried as a treatment for attention deficit hyperactivity disorder (ADHD) in adults, with mixed success. It might be especially helpful for you if depressive distractibility or indecisiveness is causing problems in your life. Please note that Wellbutrin has reportedly caused false-positive results for amphetamines in a small number of urine drug tests.

If you have epilepsy, you should not take Wellbutrin, because it can increase the risk of epileptic seizures. Ask your doctor to make sure you do not take any medications or supplements that could increase seizure risk while taking Wellbutrin. Anorexia and bulimia with purging can upset the body's mineral balance and cause seizures, so if you suffer from these problems you should not take Wellbutrin. It can also sometimes slightly increase blood pressure, and if you have a heart disease, you should probably pick a different antidepressant.

Wellbutrin comes in 75- and 100-milligram regular-release tablets that are taken three to four times daily; 100-, 150-, and 200-milligram sustained-release (SR) tablets that are taken twice a day; and 150- and 300-milligram extended-release (XR) tablets that are taken once in the morning. The regular-release and SR tablets are the largest antidepressant pills around; taking these tablets has been likened to swallowing a dime. On the other hand, Wellbutrin XR comes in trim little tablets that anyone can swallow.

Wellbutrin SR is also sold under the name of Zyban to stop the habit of cigarette smoking. If you are depressed and also want help to stop smoking, Wellbutrin may be a good antidepressant for you. It may also be helpful for other substance-use problems. Depressed cocaine abusers have stopped using cocaine after their depression was relieved by Wellbutrin.

Usual therapeutic doses range from 150 to 300 milligrams daily. You may not get a significant effect until you reach the higher doses, so do not give up if you do not feel better at low doses.

Will Zoloft make me sleepy at work?

Zoloft (generic name: sertraline) is one of the newer antidepressants that patients like most. Zoloft is called an SSRI, but studies show that it helps the brain increase serotonin at low doses, dopamine at moderate doses, and norepinephrine at higher doses. Studies also show that Zoloft stimulates the production of brain factors that help repair and regrow damaged brain cells and protect them from further damage, as many other antidepressants do. Zoloft is licensed to treat unipolar major depression, premenstrual depression, social anxiety disorder, panic disorder, and obsessive-compulsive disorder (OCD).

Patients report that Zoloft does not cause them any mental clouding or sedation. It sometimes causes a mild energizing effect, and many people prefer to take their Zoloft during the day for this reason. As sadness gradually lifts, patients report that they are able to think more clearly. Zoloft helps take away their saddest emotions and keeps negative emotions from growing. Along with relief from depression, Zoloft also may provide a reduction in irritability and anger.

My patients seldom gain weight while taking Zoloft, although they often complain of stomach and intestinal troubles right after starting the medication. These may include slight nausea, stomachache, cramping, or diarrhea. Like other serotonin antidepressants, Zoloft can delay ejaculation in men. If these problems occur, they usually get better with time and adjustment of the medication.

When you swallow your first Zoloft, it will take about six hours to get to peak levels in your system. When you stop Zoloft, all the medication and its breakdown products will be gone from your body in eight days. It comes in capsule-shaped generic tablets of 25-, 50-, and 100-milligram strengths and a menthol-scented oral solution that contains 100 milligrams per teaspoon. The Zoloft dose suggested by the *Physicians' Desk Reference* (PDR) is 50–200 milligrams per day. Occasionally patients have been prescribed 25–50 milligrams of Zoloft, but this is usually not enough to stop unipolar major depression. The most effective dose for unipolar major depression seems to be between 100–250 milligrams daily, and some studies have used 300 milligrams daily or higher.

Doctors use Zoloft for treating unipolar major depression in elders because Zoloft tends to have fewer undesirable side effects than other antidepressants. Clearance is slower in elders, and they should receive smaller doses.

What is serotonin syndrome?

Antidepressants that strongly increase levels of brain serotonin (such as SSRIs) can sometimes push the amount of serotonin too high, causing a condition cleverly called "serotonin syndrome." Mild symptoms include rapid heartbeat, sweating, dilated pupils, tremors, and twitching. There is often mental confusion, agitation, and headache. More severe symptoms include high blood pressure, overheating (hyperthermia), muscle rigidity, seizures, and coma. In extreme cases, serotonin syndrome can be fatal.

If you are taking a serotonin-stimulating antidepressant, you should consult with your doctor before using other products that stimulate serotonin, like other SSRIs, tricyclic antidepressants, monoamine oxidase inhibitors, triptans (used for treating migraines), lithium salts (used for treating bipolar disorder), opiates (including tramadol, an analgesic, and dextromethorphan, an opiate cough suppressant), Adderall or Ritalin (used for attention deficit disorder), phentermine (a diet pill), cocaine, or methamphetamine. Caution is advised when using supplements like tryptophan or St. John's wort, which may increase serotonin levels.

These problems sound scary, but in practice, serotonin syndrome from antidepressants is very rare.

What should I be aware of when taking antidepressants?

There are several important issues to keep in mind while you are taking an antidepressant.

- If an antidepressant makes you dizzy or sleepy, you should refrain from driving and take precautions to avoid falling until the problem is resolved.
- If you get a rash while taking an antidepressant, alert your doctor. Ask your doctor to examine you and tell you if the rash is likely to be caused by the medication you are taking.
- Don't drink alcohol while taking antidepressants. Alcohol can increase depression, impair sleep, and make it harder for antidepressants to work. It also may decrease the amount of antidepressant that reaches your brain.
- If you are a smoker, you should know that cigarette smoking can decrease the amount of antidepressant that reaches your brain by 30 percent. Eating grapefruit can also lower levels of some antidepressants, so check with your doctor if you are an inveterate consumer of *Citrus paradisi* (grapefruit).

- Coffee, tea, chocolate, and caffeinated drinks can make you feel shaky if you are taking antidepressants that increase norepinephrine. If you feel shaky, edgy, or agitated, try eliminating caffeine, and see if the feelings go away.
- Some medications can cause drug interactions if given together. For example, if Cymbalta is combined with the tricyclic antidepressant Norpramin, it can drive up the blood level of Norpramin by 300 percent. Make sure you check with your doctor if you are taking two or more medications at the same time.
- Antidepressants should be used cautiously if you have heart disease or hyperthyroid disorder, or if you are a diabetic. If you have heart disease, your doctor may want to give you an electrocardiogram (EKG).
- Many antidepressants that increase serotonin contain warnings about using aspirin, Motrin, and similar pain and anti-inflammatory medications that might increase the risk of bleeding. Discuss this with your doctor.
- Many antidepressants lower the seizure threshold and could cause problems if you have epilepsy.
- If you may be pregnant or are breast-feeding, do not take antidepressants without first discussing the risks and benefits with your doctors.
- Antidepressants should not be given to patients suffering from bipolar depression.
- Always check with your doctor if you have questions about your treatment.

Chapter 6

CLASSIC ANTIDEPRESSANTS

- What are tricyclic antidepressants?
- What are the differences between tricyclic antidepressants?
- What are the potential side effects of tricyclic antidepressants?
- What are the side effects of Anafranil?
- Is Elavil still prescribed?
- Is Norpramin an effective antidepressant?
- Is Pamelor measurable in the blood, and is this important?
- What are the wanted and unwanted effects of Sinequan?
- What is Tofranil?
- What are monoamine oxidase inhibitors (MAOIs)?
- What are the potential side effects of MAOIs?
- What medications should I avoid taking with my MAOI?
- What foods should I avoid while taking an MAOI?
- What if I am scheduled for surgery or a dental procedure?
- What is postural hypotension?
- Are there any other MAOI issues?
- Is there really a Band-Aid that takes away depression?
- Is Marplan still available?
- Is Nardil prescribed for the most severe depression cases?
- Why do doctors prescribe Parnate?
- Sometimes my antidepressant seems to have failed and I feel sad again—what's happening?

What are tricyclic antidepressants?

There are several reasons why you need to know about tricyclic antidepressants. Many patients prefer them to SSRIs and SNRIs, and although they are older, tricyclic antidepressants are still some of the most effective of all available antidepressants. Like the newer antidepressants, tricyclic antidepressants work by helping the brain increase serotonin, norepinephrine, and dopamine in the gaps between brain cells so the cells can fire more easily. They also increase brain factors that heal brain cells and protect the brain from the body's overactive response to stress. However, unlike SSRIs, most tricyclics increase both serotonin *and* norepinephrine, so they may have stronger effects.

Advertisements for SSRIs and SNRIs claim that they are superior to the tricyclics because they have fewer side effects like dry mouth and drowsiness, not because they are more effective at healing depression. However, tricyclics cause fewer of the side effects for which SSRIs are famous, like insomnia, anxiety, agitation, loss of sexual drive, impotence, inability to ejaculate, and numbness of the genitals. Tricyclic antidepressants have been used for years, and we know a lot about how to use them safely.

Most tricyclic antidepressants are now generic, and they are as cheap as dirt. Despite the fact that they work very well, you will not see magazine, television, or Internet advertisements extolling the virtues of these generic medications, because they are unprofitable for the major drug companies. Do not be swayed by the fact that tricyclic antidepressants are out of fashion. Like any other important decision, you have to consider the options, do your homework, and discuss the benefits and risks of the available treatment options with your doctor in order to choose the antidepressant that is right for you.

What are the differences between tricyclic antidepressants?

Each antidepressant acts and feels differently from the rest. Tricyclics also differ according to which neurochemicals they help the brain increase. You can see the relative amounts of serotonin, norepinephrine, and dopamine they stimulate in the following table. They also differ in their effects and side effects, and in how well they work to relieve depression in different people.

Characteristics of Important Tricyclic Antidepressants[1]

Name	Generic Name	Serotonin	Norepinephrine	Dopamine	Time to Leave the Body[2]
Anafranil	clomipramine	+++	++		5 days
Elavil	amitriptyline	++	++		2½ days
Norpramin	desipramine	+	++++	+	3 days
Pamelor	nortriptyline	++	+++		4 days
Sinequan	doxepin	+	++		5 days
Tofranil	imipramine	+++	+		4 days

[1] The amount of serotonin, norepinephrine, and dopamine refers to the strength of the binding to the transporter protein that is responsible for increasing serotonin, norepinephrine, and dopamine in the gap between brain cells in a chain. These values are based on data drawn from the NIMH-PDSP database and reflect a K_i range of 0–1,000 (see Appendix A, Resources).

[2] This is the amount of time it takes for 87.5 percent of the original antidepressant and/or its metabolites to leave the body. This comes from multiplying the published time it takes for one-half of the medication to leave the body times three.

What are the potential side effects of tricyclic antidepressants?

Tricyclic antidepressants and many other medications share a group of side effects that are caused by blocking the neurochemicals called acetylcholine (ACh) and histamine (HIST) in the brain. These symptoms are commonly referred to as "anticholinergic effects." Early in the history of antidepressants, anticholinergic effects were thought to play an important part in reducing depression, but nowadays they are just considered a bother. Anticholinergic effects are strongest in Elavil, Anafranil, and Sinequan, and weaker in Norpramin, Tofranil, and Pamelor.

If you have a cold or allergy, anticholinergic effects will dry up your watery nose, open your congested sinuses, reduce your cough, and keep your eyes from being red and watery. They will probably reduce your seasickness symptoms as well. However, if you do not have a cold, allergy, or seasickness, you may not appreciate the dry mouth, dry eyes, decreased perspiration, weight gain, and increased tendency toward constipation that are caused by the antidepressants with the strongest anticholinergic effects. At high doses of Elavil or Anafranil, you might even have temporarily blurred vision or difficulty urinating. Elders may have an increased risk for falls and clouded thinking, especially if their antidepressant dose is too high.

Strongly anticholinergic antidepressants produce a sedative effect, which can make you feel relaxed or drowsy, depending on your viewpoint. Anticholinergic antidepressants make it easier to go to sleep at night, but depending on the antidepressant and the dose, you may feel drowsy during the day.

At high doses, strongly anticholinergic antidepressants produce a feeling of distance from current activities, sometimes likened to seeing the world through a thick pane of glass. If your conscious mind is currently filled with pain and misery, this distance can be a great relief. If negative thoughts are bombarding your mind and you cannot stop them, tricyclics can slow them down and keep your thoughts from going too far in painful or dangerous directions. However, if you are trying to write a book or do your taxes, this feeling of mild detachment is a nuisance. Many allergy and cold products such as Benadryl (diphenhydramine) produce similar effects.

Anticholinergic effects may increase your appetite. If you have not been able to eat anything and you have lost so much weight that you are gaunt, tricyclics can make it easier to get back to normal eating patterns. Otherwise, you may tend to gain weight, and you will have to watch what you eat.

Fortunately, these anticholinergic effects diminish over time. In the meantime, keeping a fresh water bottle handy protects you from dry mouth, and psyllium supplements (like Metamucil) will help prevent constipation while lowering your cholesterol levels. Drinking a little coffee, tea, or a soft drink can help counteract any daytime sleepiness you may encounter.

Tricyclic antidepressants have a few other side effects that you should be aware of. Norepinephrine brain cells contain a special class of switches called norepinephrine alpha-1 receptors. When norepinephrine antidepressants turn on these switches, you may be more likely to become dizzy or fall if you stand or sit up quickly. This effect is called postural hypotension, and it affects some individuals more than others. Until you find out whether you are vulnerable, you should be careful not to rise suddenly from a lying, sitting, bent over, or kneeling position when you are starting a classic antidepressant. Before you stand up, grab a solid object for support, and count to ten as you rise slowly. If you find yourself suffering from postural hypotension, know that the effect usually declines over a few days to weeks. Until then, drink plenty of fluids and consume extra salt to help keep your blood pressure from dropping when you rise.

Tricyclic antidepressants may also worsen heart disease, if you have any heart problems. Ask your psychiatrist and primary care doctor about the cardiac effects of tricyclic antidepressants.

What are the side effects of Anafranil?

Anafranil (generic name: clomipramine) was developed in the 1960s by the Swiss manufacturer Geigy, now known as Novartis. It helps increase brain serotonin at low doses and norepinephrine at moderate doses. Anafranil may be especially helpful in the treatment of obsessive-compulsive disorder (OCD) or panic disorder. It comes in 25-, 50-, and 75-milligram capsules and is usually started at 25 milligrams at bedtime, gradually increasing to 75–225 milligrams. It stays in the body four to six days after you stop taking it.

Anafranil works very well at decreasing depression, but because of its strong side effects—dry mouth, dry eyes, sedation, constipation, and weight gain—many patients do not like it. There are other tricyclic antidepressants, like Tofranil, that are just as effective but have fewer side effects. Interestingly, clomipramine is sold by veterinarians under the name Clomicalm, as a treatment for obsessive habits like skin licking and tail chasing.

Is Elavil still prescribed?

Elavil (generic name: amitriptyline) is the hoary, white-bearded grandfather of tricyclic antidepressants; it's been around forever, and we know lots about it. It helps the body increase both serotonin and norepinephrine, and studies have repeatedly shown that Elavil is an effective medicine for depression. Patients say it stops them from overthinking on negative topics and dulls all their emotions, providing a rest from depression. Although it is not licensed for this use, Elavil is often used to treat diabetic pain, to treat muscle and joint pain, or to prevent migraine headaches (although it will not stop a migraine after it has started).

At doses high enough to treat depression, Elavil always makes you feel very sleepy. There is a feeling of distance from events around you, like the feeling Sylvia Plath wrote about in *The Bell Jar* (see Appendix A, Resources). It's been described as "looking at the world through the wrong end of a pair of binoculars." This feeling is very much like the side effects of antihistaminic allergy or cold medicines. The effect decreases with time, but it may never go away entirely.

Most people find that Elavil makes them both thirsty and constipated. Weight gain is another major side effect of Elavil. Sometimes it seems that just walking past a bottle of it is enough to add on a few pounds. Elavil is also well known for causing falls if you should sit or stand up too quickly (postural hypotension). Falling is especially important to avoid in elder adults, who may break their hips or experience other life-threatening consequences after a fall.

Elavil comes in 10-, 25-, 50-, 75-, 100-, and 150-milligram tablets. It is usually started at a low dose of 25–50 milligrams at bedtime, because of the strong side effects it causes. I rarely see doses above 150 milligrams, for the same reason. The first dose of Elavil takes about four hours to reach its maximum concentration in your body, and it stays in your bloodstream for about two and a half days after your last dose.

Despite the fact that Elavil is a popular antidepressant with doctors, it has too many strong side effects for most patients.

Is Norpramin an effective antidepressant?

Norpramin (generic name: desipramine) is one of the best antidepressants ever made. It helps the body strongly increase norepinephrine in the gaps between brain cells at low doses, and it has some effect on serotonin and dopamine at higher doses. Like other antidepressants, studies have shown that Norpramin can increase the brain cell–healing factor called BDNF.

Although it is not licensed for this use, Norpramin (as well as other medications that increase norepinephrine) is effective at preventing migraine headaches and the pain that arises from nerve damage in diabetes. It is often used to treat chronic pain in the neck, shoulders, and lower back. Norpramin works well for individuals who have severe pain on the soles of their feet from alcoholism.

Patients say that Norpramin reduces their darkest emotions; you can still feel their presence, but they are in the background and do not seem as painful. Norpramin helps keep patients from overthinking and making mountains out of molehills. It has a slight dulling effect on sadness, anger, anxiety, and other emotions. Norpramin produces fewer anticholinergic side effects (like daytime sleepiness, dry mouth, or constipation) than the other tricyclic antidepressants. Many people are happy taking Norpramin all their lives and prefer it to SSRIs and other more modern medications they have tried.

Norpramin comes in 10-, 25-, 75-, 100-, and 150-milligram tablets. It is usually started at 25–50 milligrams at bedtime and increased to 150–300 milligrams daily. After taking Norpramin, it will take about five hours to reach its peak concentration in your bloodstream. After reaching a steady level in the bloodstream, it takes about three days to leave the body.

Based on patients' comments, Norpramin is one of the best antidepressants. Many depressed patients show their first response to treatment only after Norpramin is added. It may trigger mania in patients with bipolar disorder, so it should be avoided in patients with this illness.

Is Pamelor measurable in the blood, and is this important?

Pamelor (generic name: nortriptyline) helps the brain increase norepinephrine at low doses and serotonin at medium doses. It is licensed for depression and is sometimes prescribed for migraine and chronic pain. There are reports that Pamelor can reduce ringing in the ears (tinnitus).

Unlike most antidepressants, there is a laboratory blood test that can show how much Pamelor is in your bloodstream. However, the amount of Pamelor in your blood cannot determine whether you need more or less Pamelor to help with your depression; only you and your doctor can tell that.

Side effects include the usual tricyclic suspects like dry eyes, dry mouth, dry mucous membranes, low blood pressure when standing (postural hypotension), constipation, and difficulty urinating. Pamelor reaches a peak in your bloodstream eight hours after you take it and stays in your body four days after your last dose. It comes in 10-, 25-, and 50-milligram capsules. Pamelor doses are about one-half the usual doses for other tricyclic antidepressants, starting at 25 milligrams and increasing to 100 milligrams. The usual maximum dose is 150 milligrams.

Other than the laboratory test, most patients have not found any particular advantages of Pamelor over the most effective tricyclic antidepressants.

What are the wanted and unwanted effects of Sinequan?

Sinequan (generic name: doxepin) is an elderly antidepressant that helps the brain increase norepinephrine at moderate doses and serotonin at higher doses. Sinequan is quite good for depression with insomnia, weight loss, or irritability. It is used to treat unipolar major depression as well as anxiety, organic depression resulting from brain injury, depression caused by alcoholism, and psychotic depression. Sinequan also provides great benefits for people with heartburn or acid reflux, because it decreases the secretion of stomach acid. The liquid form is anesthetic, and it cools stomach pain on contact. Sinequan also can prevent migraine headaches, reduce pain resulting from diabetes and nerve damage, and minimize chronic pain in the neck, shoulders, and lower back (although it is not licensed for this purpose). Many patients like Sinequan and find it very effective.

Patients say that Sinequan keeps their negative emotions from escalating and their negative thoughts from going too far afield. It creates a slight dulling effect that is a great relief if your mind is overflowing with painful emotions and intrusive negative thoughts. Even at low doses, Sinequan can help improve your sleep. In fact, pharmaceutical companies are debating whether to release low-dose Sinequan as the sleeping tablet of the future.

On the downside, Sinequan is usually sedating during the day, at least at first. Sedation can be avoided or minimized by increasing the dose slowly and allowing your body to adjust. Sinequan can also cause weight gain, so it is important to watch your diet. It can make some people dizzy if they stand up quickly, so it is important to watch for this, especially in the first few weeks.

One advantage of Sinequan is that it can be given in very low doses to expose you to as few side effects as possible. For example, Sinequan is made in 10- and 25-milligram capsules (as well as 50-, 75-, 100-, and 150-milligram sizes), although your pharmacist may not have all the sizes in stock. Sinequan is also available in an unflavored liquid form that is easy to take. It delivers 50 milligrams per teaspoonful, and it comes with a dropper that can measure smaller doses.

You usually start Sinequan at 10–25 milligrams and increase it to between 75 and 150 milligrams. Some patients may require higher doses (200–250 milligrams) to quell their depressive symptoms. After you stop taking Sinequan, it clears from your body in about two days. Some Sinequan is metabolized into the antidepressant called desmethyldoxepin, which stays around as many as five days. Sinequan is not recommended for elder adults, because its typical tricyclic antidepressant side effects may cause a risk of falls, sedation, or confusion.

What is Tofranil?

Tofranil (generic name: imipramine) is the best of the tricyclic antidepressants. Studies show that it is as good as or better than any of the modern antidepressants, and many patients prefer it to SSRIs and SNRIs. Some patients say that of all the antidepressants they've tried, they had the fewest depressive symptoms while taking Tofranil.

Tofranil helps the brain increase serotonin at low doses and norepinephrine at medium doses. It has been around a long time, and we know a lot about it—it was the first tricyclic antidepressant to be synthesized in the late 1940s by chemists looking for new pain and allergy medications. For a long time, Tofranil was considered the gold standard to which all other antidepressants were compared. Tofranil may work so well because it closely matches the chemical deficits that occur in depression; it may be the most chemically accurate treatment.

Patients say that Tofranil stops their negative thoughts from progressing and worsening. It also prevents unhappy emotions from progressing and getting more painful, and it removes patients' saddest, most negative emotions. Most people will experience some symptoms of dry mouth, sedation, or mild constipation, at least at first. Tofranil causes a tendency to gain weight, but most people can remain slim by watching their diet.

In contrast with the SSRIs, Tofranil rarely makes people anxious, keeps them from sleeping, or causes sexual complaints. The mild sedation caused by Tofranil can decrease anxiety and help people relax and go to sleep. It comes in 10-, 25-, and 50-milligram tablets and 75-, 100-, 125-, and 150-milligram capsules. Tofranil reaches its peak concentration in the bloodstream about four hours after you swallow it, and it's gone from the body in about four days. Tofranil stays around longer in elder adults, who should receive smaller doses.

You will usually start Tofranil at 25–50 milligrams at bedtime and increase every one to two weeks until you reach 200 milligrams. Then wait and reassess the situation; if warranted, you can increase the dose up to 300 milligrams.

What are monoamine oxidase inhibitors (MAOIs)?

Monoamine oxidase inhibitors (MAOIs) were introduced in the early 1950s. These antidepressants strongly increase serotonin, norepinephrine, *and* dopamine in the depressed brain; perhaps this is why MAOIs work so well.

Monoamine oxidase (MAO) is the brain enzyme that disposes of extra serotonin, norepinephrine, and dopamine so they do not build up in the brain. In depressed individuals, whose brain cells have been damaged by stress, MAO breaks down so much serotonin, norepinephrine, and dopamine that there is not enough to allow brain cells to fire normally. MAO inhibitors (MAOIs) block this enzyme so that more serotonin, norepinephrine, and dopamine are available to your brain cells and they can again carry signals through your brain. Many doctors consider some of the monoamine oxidase inhibitors to be the best antidepressants ever marketed.

MAOIs also reverse some of the natural changes of aging in the brain. Can MAOIs keep your brain young? We do not yet know the answer, but it is an interesting possibility.

What are the potential side effects of MAOIs?

There are a few side effects that you should know about if you're considering taking an MAOI. Hypertensive crisis is a sudden, rapid, extreme, and potentially fatal increase in blood pressure that can occur when patients combine MAOIs (Nardil, Parnate, Marplan, or high-dose EMSAM) with certain other medications, foods, or beverages. If you take an MAOI, you should ask your doctor about a quick-working medication to reduce blood pressure (such as nifedipine or clonidine) that you can carry with you in case you experience a hypertensive crisis. Discuss this in length with your doctor, and make sure you have a list of what you can and cannot take before you start a monoamine oxidase inhibitor.

What medications should I avoid taking with my MAOI?

In order to avoid hypertensive crisis, individuals who are taking MAOIs such as Nardil, Marplan, Parnate, or high-dose EMSAM must avoid taking

- other antidepressants
- asthma medicines like Tornalate (bitolerol) Seravent (salme-terol), Primatene (epinephrine), Uniphyl (theophylline), and other bronchial dilators
- narcotic pain medicines like Demerol (meperidine), tramadol, methadone, or propoxyphene
- over-the-counter cold or cough medications that contain dextromethorphan (which is related to narcotic pain medicines)

- Flexeril (cyclobenzaprine; a muscle relaxant with a structure like an antidepressant)
- Strattera (atomoxetine; a medication for attention deficit hyperactivity disorder with a structure like an antidepressant)
- stimulants used to treat attention deficit hyperactivity disorder such as Ritalin (methylphenidate), Dexedrine (dextroamphetamine), and Adderall (mixed amphetamine salts)
- guanethidine, methyldopa, reserpine, dopamine, or levodopa.
- BuSpar (buspirone; an anxiety medication)
- seizure medications like Tegretol (carbamazepine) and Trileptal (oxcarbazepine)
- supplements containing St. John's wort, tyramine, or tryptophan
- methamphetamine or cocaine
- prescription or over-the-counter weight loss products, decongestants, or cough and cold medicines without clearing them with your doctor
- any other substances your doctor advises you to avoid

What foods should I avoid while taking an MAOI?

Ask your doctor to provide a list of foods for you to avoid. Usually the offending foods are fermented like yeast extract or aged like cheese. Meat, fish, and chicken products that have been aged, pickled, fermented, or smoked should be avoided. Avoid foods thought to be high in tyramine, which can trigger a high blood pressure crisis. Following is a general list of foods your doctor may ask you to avoid:

- anchovies
- ripe or fermented avocados

- bacon
- beer (including nonalcoholic beer)
- canned prunes or figs
- caviar
- strong or aged cheese
- Chianti, port, sherry, and other wines
- distilled alcoholic beverages
- dried fruits like raisins and prunes
- aged dry ham
- meat extracts
- meat prepared with tenderizers
- pickled herring
- rice vinegar
- sake
- sauerkraut
- aged dry sausage
- sour cream
- soy sauce
- yeast extracts such as Marmite or Bovril
- yogurt

It is a good idea to stop using these medicines and eating these foods a week or more before starting to use Nardil, Parnate, Marplan, or high-dose EMSAM. Continue to avoid them for at least two weeks after stopping your MAO inhibitor. Because of these restrictions, MAOIs should only be given to patients who are able to follow the list of medication and dietary restrictions faithfully. Make sure you have discussed these side effects at length with your doctor, and make sure you have a list of what you can and cannot take before you start any MAOI.

What if I am scheduled for surgery or a dental procedure?

You should usually stop MAOIs before medical or dental operations requiring general anesthetics, or local anesthetics containing epinephrine. Tell your surgeon, anesthesiologist, and dentist as soon as possible that you are taking an MAOI, and follow their directions.

What is postural hypotension?

Monoamine oxidase inhibitors, particularly Nardil, can cause your blood pressure to drop when you stand up, which we call postural hypotension. If you stand or sit up quickly, you may become dizzy, feel uncoordinated, black out, or fall. This may occur when sitting up or rising from bed, standing up from a chair, or standing up after kneeling or bending down. Until you know whether you will have this side effect, it is important not to rise suddenly from sitting, lying, or bending-down positions. Always remember to sit or stand up slowly with your hand on a solid object for support so you will not fall if you become dizzy or black out. This side effect usually decreases with time.

Are there any other MAOI issues?

Monoamine oxidase inhibitors may cause muscle jerks, numbness, and tingling or electric sensations called paresthesias, especially at bedtime. These usually go away or decrease significantly over a few days to weeks. MAOIs should not be used if you suffer from bipolar disorder, congestive heart failure, liver disease, seizure disorder, hyperthyroid disorder, or diabetes. Do not take monoamine oxidase inhibitors if you may become pregnant or are breast-feeding.

After stopping MAOIs, they are usually gone from the body quickly, but their MAO inhibition continues for one to two weeks.

This is why it is necessary to keep observing the medication and dietary restrictions for two weeks or more after stopping. For the same reason, monoamine oxidase inhibitors should be discontinued for at least three weeks before starting another antidepressant. Check with your doctor for more details.

Many physicians have never used monoamine oxidase inhibitors and are afraid to try them. There have even been cases where severely depressed patients' MAOIs have been summarily discontinued when they went into the hospital because no physician there had any experience with their use. MAOIs are not even being taught in some medical schools anymore. This is too bad, because with all their warts and limitations, MAOIs have been known to quell the worst depression imaginable.

Is there really a Band-Aid that takes away depression?

EMSAM (generic names: selegiline and deprenyl) is the first antidepressant available in the form of a patch that looks like a Band-Aid. To make EMSAM, the medication selegiline is mixed with tacky plastics—acrylic, ethylene vinyl acetate, polyethylene, polyester, polyurethane, and silicon-coated polyester—and applied to the back of a plastic square. When you unwrap the patch and stick it onto your skin, it releases selegiline into your body for twenty-four hours. The most common side effect of EMSAM is irritation of the skin under the patch.

EMSAM patches come in three sizes that deliver 6, 9, or 12 milligrams of selegiline per day. At the 6-milligram dose, EMSAM is free from the potentially fatal high blood pressure reaction to foods and other medications. Unfortunately, EMSAM is not very effective for depression at this low dose.

The higher dose 9- and 12-milligram EMSAM patches are more effective at reducing depression, but at these doses, you must avoid the MAOI list of proscribed medications and foods. If not, the 9- or 12-milligram patches can trigger potentially fatal attacks of high blood pressure like other MAOIs. Because other MAOIs like Nardil, and Parnate carry similar risks and work much better for depression, EMSAM does not fare well on a risk/benefit comparison, and many patients do not like EMSAM.

Is Marplan still available?

Marplan (generic name: isocarboxazid) is an MAOI that has been around for many years but gradually fell out of use. Now a pharmaceutical company has taken Marplan under its wing and is trying to bring it back.

Marplan works the same way as other MAOIs, by blocking the enzyme that destroys serotonin, norepinephrine, and dopamine. It also has similar side effects. Doctors who swear by Marplan say that it is less sedating and less likely to cause postural hypotension than Nardil. It is less stimulating than Parnate. Marplan comes in 10-milligram tablets and is typically started at one tablet twice daily.

One big reservation doctors have about Marplan is the danger of prescribing an antidepressant that might go off the market and become unavailable. If Marplan becomes more popular again, it will likely come into more widespread use.

Is Nardil prescribed for the most severe depression cases?

Nardil (generic name: phenelzine) is one of the most effective antidepressants ever developed. It can alleviate depression in many individuals whose unipolar major depression has not been helped by any other antidepressants. For the most part, Nardil makes people feel like their most natural selves, without any particular coloration other than a feeling of increased relaxation and calm. Like other MAOIs, Nardil increases the amount of serotonin, norepinephrine, and dopamine in the gaps between brain cells by inhibiting the enzyme that usually breaks the neurochemicals down.

People take Nardil because it works, not because it is free of side effects. It can cause postural hypotension and the potentially fatal condition called hypertensive crisis if you combine it with the wrong medicines or foods. In some people, Nardil can cause sedation, daytime sleepiness, and/or insomnia, which usually decrease with time. Nardil usually causes sexual problems, which may lessen with time. Nardil often causes weight gain, though many patients taking Nardil are quite thin. Some people never experience any side effects at all.

Nardil comes in 15-milligram tablets; you usually start at one tablet daily and increase every week to a maximum of three tablets daily (45 milligrams). After your depression is gone, the dose can often be reduced. Check with your doctor for more details.

In addition to being licensed to treat unipolar major depression, Nardil is also effective for anxiety, social anxiety disorder, obsessive-compulsive disorder, and other conditions for which it is not licensed. It should never be given to patients suffering from bipolar disorder. If you are interested in Nardil, discuss it with your psychiatrist.

Why do doctors prescribe Parnate?

Parnate (generic name: tranylcypromine) may be the most effective antidepressant ever made. Parnate increases the concentrations of serotonin, norepinephrine, and dopamine throughout the nervous system. It also increases the levels of the brain-healing factor called BDNF, particularly in the area of the brain called the hippocampus, which is damaged by depression. Parnate heals the depression of many "treatment-resistant" individuals who have not responded to any of the other antidepressants. Although not licensed for these uses, Parnate is quite effective in patients with combined depression and anxiety, as well as social anxiety disorder, obsessive-compulsive disorder, and other conditions.

Patients say that Parnate usually makes them feel more like themselves, with the addition of some extra energy. If you have been feeling unnaturally depressed for a long time, this transition can be breathtaking. Unlike Nardil, Parnate is usually activating and alerting, and so it can get you up and moving while improving your attention (although a few people experience sedation instead). Compared with Nardil, Parnate is unlikely to cause weight gain or sexual problems. In some people, Parnate's activation may turn into sleep problems, especially early in the course of treatment. Avoid consuming caffeinated drinks or chocolate, because these can combine with the activating effects of Parnate to make your hands shake and your heart race.

Like other MAOIs, Parnate can cause a severe and possibly fatal increase in blood pressure if it is taken in combination with the wrong medications and foods and so it should not be the first antidepressant that you try. It can also cause dizziness and falling if you stand up suddenly, although less so than Nardil. The usual starting dose is 10 milligrams in the morning, which can be increased to 30 milligrams or more over the course of one to two months at the discretion of your doctor.

Parnate is only sold in 10-milligram tablets, which is irritatingly inconvenient if you need to take several of them daily. GlaxoSmithKline, the makers of Parnate, have no interest in promoting the drug, and higher-dose pills are unlikely. It is very unfortunate that today's new doctors often fail to consider giving

Parnate to their severely depressed patients; it's a very effective antidepressant.

Sometimes my antidepressant seems to have failed and I feel sad again—what's happening?

You need to understand how depression goes away. Instead of just feeling better and better with time, you begin by feeling better in short episodes. As your depression continues to heal, these "undepressed" episodes grow longer and closer together until you feel better for days at a time. You will begin to retain a feeling of happiness and normalcy for weeks, then months at a time until you almost forget what your depression was like.

However, when you do have a moment of depression, the feelings will still be strong. Don't panic if the bad memories and dark associations come back briefly in full force. This does not mean your treatment is not working, nor does it mean that you are falling back into depression. This is just the way depression makes its exit, with brief curtain calls that grow shorter and farther apart.

Chapter 7

WHAT IF YOUR ANTIDEPRESSANT DOESN'T WORK?

- Will it be necessary for me to try more than one antidepressant?
- My depression is 80–90 percent gone—is that good enough?
- What do I do if I'm taking an antidepressant but I still feel depressed?
- Is it better to suffer a little to keep the dosage as low as possible?
- What should I do if my antidepressant just isn't working?
- What is BuSpar?
- Why would you want to give me an antipsychotic for depression?
- What is Zyprexa?
- Is Geodon effective in treating depression?
- Is Seroquel a sleeping pill?
- What is Risperdal?
- Is Stelazine still available?
- What are mood stabilizers, and how can they help my depression?
- Do tranquilizers have a place in treating depression?
- Are new drugs being developed to treat depression?
- Is there any way a medication could turn off stress?
- Is depression caused by brain inflammation that can be treated with aspirin?
- What is the newest development in modern antidepressants?
- Are doctors testing medications used for Parkinson's disease to see if they treat depression?
- Will there be any new MAOIs?
- I read there is a new combined sleep and antidepressant medication coming up. What is it?
- Is there any medical way to cure depression without medication?
- Can depression be eliminated with magnets?
- Is there a pacemaker on the market that stops depression?
- How does convulsant therapy work for depression?
- Are these alternative treatments safe?

Will it be necessary for me to try more than one antidepressant?

This all depends on how good you and your psychiatrist are at selecting antidepressants. With a good doctor-patient relationship, good information, and some luck, you will find the best antidepressant on the first try. Then it is just a matter of finding the perfect dose and adjusting it over the course of weeks or months. If you are not happy with the results or you find that there are still depressive problems left after you have reached your highest dose, then you may need to change your treatment strategy.

My depression is 80–90 percent gone—is that good enough?

Although it can be a big relief when your most painful depressive symptoms fade, the ultimate goal of treatment is to eliminate *all* your depressive symptoms. Surprisingly, it may not be easy to tell when your episode of unipolar major depression is finally over. If you have been depressed for a long time, you may make the mistake of thinking that some of your depressive symptoms are part of your nature and not the disease. Many of my patients have thought their depression was over, but when we increased their medications, they found that they had still been somewhat depressed. You need to persist aggressively in your treatment until you are sure you feel like your most normal and natural self.

What do I do if I'm taking an antidepressant but I still feel depressed?

Check the dose of your antidepressant, and make sure you have been taking it long enough for it to work. A study showed that 85 percent of depressed patients never received adequate relief because their antidepressant doses were too low or their antidepressants had not had enough time to work. Obviously, if you have to increase the medication dose slowly to minimize side effects, then it may take several weeks to reach an effective dose, but some antidepressants can be started at their optimum dose (like Paxil or Prozac), which saves a lot of time. According to most authorities, you should take an antidepressant for six to eight weeks at the highest recommended dose before giving up on that medicine.

Is it better to suffer a little to keep the dosage as low as possible?

This is probably a mistake; there's no reason to suffer unnecessarily. The goal of medication treatment is to squelch your depression, not to keep you from taking medications. Unless higher doses cause intolerable side effects or endanger your health, the best and safest approach is to use the dose that completely eliminates your depressive symptoms, as long you are not taking more than the maximum recommended dose (see chapters 5 and 6 on antidepressants). Check with your doctor and the *Physician's Desk Reference* (PDR, see Appendix A, Resources) to find the maximum recommended dose for the medication you're taking.

What should I do if my antidepressant just isn't working?

If you have been taking your antidepressant at an adequate dose for a sufficient time and it still is not working, get together with your doctor and form a new plan of attack. Here are several good strategies to try:

Plan A: Change the Antidepressant

If you are taking a serotonin antidepressant like Celexa or Lexapro, consider changing to a norepinephrine antidepressant like Norpramin, a dopamine antidepressant like Wellbutrin, or a mixed serotonin/ norepinephrine antidepressant like Effexor or Tofranil. You can make this change in two ways, either by completely stopping the old antidepressant and then starting the new one, or by decreasing the old while increasing the new antidepressant at the same time. The second option may be preferable, because it provides you with some protection against uncontrolled depression at all times.

Another option is to stop the first antidepressant, wait several weeks until it is gone from your body, and start a monoamine oxidase inhibitor (MAOI). As discussed, MAOIs work very well, but they are difficult to manage and potentially dangerous. They should not be among your first choices.

Plan B: Add a Second Antidepressant

This plan provides you with a win-win situation: If you add the new antidepressant to your current antidepressant and you feel better, then you have accomplished your goal. If the new antidepressant does not help or you do not like it, then you can simply take it away, and you will be no worse off than before.

If the new antidepressant seems to be improving your depression, you can increase the dose until you are getting the maximum benefit from the new medication. Then you can either taper away the old medication or keep both if you find that you need them for adequate depression relief. For instance, if Effexor was not relieving all your symptoms, you could add Desyrel for increased serotonin effects, Norpramin for increased norepinephrine effects, or Wellbutrin for increased dopamine effects. Each of those choices complements your current antidepressant in a different way. Ask your doctor to make sure that you choose a second antidepressant that does not have any undesirable drug interactions with the first one.

Plan C: Add a Low Dose of Another Medication as an Adjuvant

An adjuvant is the name for a second medication that is added to the first to enhance its effectiveness. In the case of depression, an adjuvant may entail starting a low dose of another antidepressant (like 10–50 milligrams of Desyrel, Tofranil, Sinequan, or Norpramin) to your current antidepressant to make it work better. It could be the addition of a low dose of an antipsychotic like Geodon, a mood stabilizer like lithium salt or Tegretol, or a sedative like Ativan or Xanax. Always ask your doctor to make sure there are no undesirable drug interactions between your antidepressant and the new medication.

Plan C allows you to start a new treatment at a low dose to see whether it benefits you. If it is not helpful, you can discontinue it without being exposed to any risks or discomfort that might accompany a higher dose. If the adjuvant proves helpful, you can leave good enough alone or gradually increase the dose of the adjuvant.

For example, if you are taking Zoloft with little success, you might add a low dose of Norpramin to increase norepinephrine effects. If your depression symptoms start to diminish, you could increase the Norpramin dose to see if you continue to improve. At the Norpramin dose where you stop improving, you can stop or see if you could taper away some or all of the Zoloft.

Many depressed patients respond best to two medications. Sometimes two antidepressants can be taken at lower doses rather than taking one medication at a higher dose with more side effects. Make sure you and your doctor discuss what you plan to do in advance and proceed in an orderly, scientific, and methodical way. Never bounce back and forth blindly from antidepressant to antidepressant without following a plan.

You should know that the prospect of taking two or more medications simultaneously sometimes drives university professors and recent medical graduates nuts, because they are taught to use only one medication at a time.

What is BuSpar?

BuSpar (buspirone) is a medication intended for the treatment of anxiety and depression. It works by turning on a receptor switch located on the surface of serotonin brain cells called the serotonin-1A receptor. Studies show that BuSpar can relieve both depressive and anxious symptoms, but the effect is not large. Doctors sometimes add BuSpar to existing antidepressants to increase their effects, but BuSpar is seldom sufficiently effective on its own.

Why would you want to give me an antipsychotic for depression?

Antipsychotics are typically used at high doses in severe disorders like schizophrenia, but some of them have antidepressant effects, particularly at low doses. When added to antidepressants, they can provide a second line of defense against unipolar major depression. As their name suggests, antipsychotics are particularly useful in psychotic depression where, for example, the depressed person has unreasonable, paranoid fears. As a bonus, they are often relaxing and promote sleep. For other information on psychotic depression, see Chapter 16, When All Else Fails. Most antipsychotics are not licensed for treating depression.

What is Zyprexa?

Zyprexa (generic name: olanzapine) is one of the strongest of the current generation of antipsychotics. It is usually somewhat sedating. Zyprexa's worst drawback is its tendency to cause significant weight gain; unchecked, large gains in body weight increase your risk for other health problems including diabetes and heart disease. Weight gain from Zyprexa may be less if you take the rapid dissolving Zydis formulation. In the treatment of unipolar major depression, Zyprexa can be used successfully at very low doses to minimize side effects. Zyprexa can also be used to help depressed patients gain weight after they have become too gaunt from loss of appetite.

Is Geodon effective in treating depression?

Right now, Geodon (generic name: ziprasidone) is one of the most useful antipsychotics in the treatment of unipolar major depression. Patients say it is not sedating and it does not make them gain weight. It has antidepressant properties, and it is often effective at the lowest dose, when added to antidepressants. Like many other medicines, it may rarely increase the chances of heart arrhythmia, so do not take it if you have heart disease.

Is Seroquel a sleeping pill?

Seroquel (generic name: quetiapine) is another antipsychotic that is sedating and can cause moderate weight gain. In addition to Desyrel, many doctors offer Seroquel to their depressed patients for sleep because it is effective at tiny doses, it is not at all addictive, and research studies have demonstrated that Seroquel can sometimes help relieve unipolar major depression when added to antidepressants. (Neither Desyrel nor Seroquel are licensed as sleeping medications.)

What is Risperdal?

Although Risperdal (generic name: risperidone) is sometimes offered to depressed patients, it can cause restlessness and involuntary movements, albeit rarely, and it causes moderate weight gain. People with depression, for some reason, are prescribed this medication with some frequency; unless your doctor gives you a specific reason that this is the best medication for you, you should probably refuse it.

Is Stelazine still available?

Stelazine (generic name: trifluoperazine) is an older antipsychotic that has antidepressant properties and can often improve treatment when added to antidepressants at low doses of 1–5 milligrams per day. It can potentially cause restlessness and temporary or permanent involuntary movements. Otherwise, patients say that Stelazine is not sedating and they do not gain weight if they watch their diets. Several depressed patients have told me they find Stelazine more effective than Zyprexa. If you are interested in Stelazine, discuss its risks and benefits thoroughly with your doctor before trying it.

What are mood stabilizers, and how can they help my depression?

Mood stabilizers are medications that are usually used to treat epilepsy and bipolar disorder. The addition of a mood stabilizer has helped some people get more relief from their antidepressant. Escalith and Lithobid (lithium salts) are also known to reduce the risk of suicide.

Escalith and Lithobid, Equetro and Tegretol (carbamazepine), and Depakote (sodium valproate) increase the brain-derived neurotrophic factor (BDNF) that helps to repair damaged brain cells and protect brain cells from stress. Lamictal (lamotrigine) and Topamax (topiramate) can reduce your brain's reaction to stress by other mechanisms.

Mood stabilizers can have potentially fatal side effects and need to be managed closely by your doctor. They are usually not licensed for treating unipolar major depression. If you want to use them, discuss their risks and benefits with your doctor first.

Do tranquilizers have a place in treating depression?

Although they are not licensed for this use, sedatives like Ambien (zolpidem), Ativan (lorazepam), Klonopin (clonazepam), Valium (diazepam), and Xanax (alprazolam) are often prescribed to depressed individuals who complain of anxiety, agitation, or insomnia.

There are many good reasons to refuse sedatives. For example, all sedatives are potentially addictive. They can increase sadness, irritability, anger, and impulsive behaviors such as suicide, aggression, binge drinking, and inappropriate drug use. Studies have shown that people who take sedatives may not even be aware that they are more irritable and angry. Sedatives also impair learning, sabotage memory, and interfere with mental processes. The situation may be worse if you take sedatives for a long time. After you finally stop taking sedatives, the mental deficits they cause may take over six months to go away.

Some patients have had psychotic episodes with the latest sleeping medicines. Sedatives can also cause failure of the breathing response and death if taken in overdose or with alcohol.

Insomnia is one of the diagnostic symptoms of unipolar major depression. If one of my patients is sleeping poorly, my first step is to strengthen their depression treatment and help them improve their sleeping habits. If an additional medication is necessary for sleeping, I suggest starting with low doses of Benadryl (diphenhydramine, an over-the-counter antihistamine allergy medicine). The antidepressant Desyrel (trazodone) makes people sleepy during the night, and I often use it as both an antidepressant and a treatment for insomnia.

You should know that it is very common now for medical doctors to prescribe sedatives like Valium or Xanax to the bereaved. This is a well-meaning gesture, but sedatives can interfere with the process of recovery from grief. It is quite annoying to wake up from a few months of medical fog to find that you still have your grief recovery period ahead of you. Worse, sedatives can make people more depressed and more likely to have accidents and perform impulsive behaviors like suicide.

Are new drugs being developed to treat depression?

Right now, pharmaceutical companies are in a race to evaluate current and new medications in the hopes that they can develop the next, most effective, best-selling new antidepressant. There is an enormous amount of money at stake, so you can be sure that pharmaceutical companies are working around the clock.

Some of the potential antidepressants being worked on, if successful, will change the future of depression treatment. You can follow new medications through the stages of testing and licensure by visiting http://www.clintrials.gov or by typing their names or code numbers into www.dogpile.com or your favorite search engine.

New Medications: The Wave of the Future

Antidepressant Type	Action[2]	Examples[1]
Anti-Stress Antidepressants	Increases BDNF	Rolipram, Cistamine, RO-20-1724
	Turns Off NMDA Receptors	Namenda, Rilutek, Mifeprex, AZD-6765, TIK-101
	Turns Off Glucocorticoid Receptors	ORG-34517
	Turns off Corticotropin Releasing Factor	Antalarmin, Pexacerfont, CP-154526, GSK-876008, NBI-27914, NBI-30545, ONO-2333, SSR-126374

	Turns off Vasopressin Receptors	SSR-149415
Anti-inflammatory Antidepressants	Turns Off Neurokinin Receptors	Casopitant, Orvepitant, RP-67580, SR-140333
Triple Reuptake Inhibitor Antidepressants	Increases Serotonin, Norepinephrine, Dopamine	DOV-102677, DOV-21947, GSK-372475, SEP-225289
Dopamine Antidepressants	Increases Dopamine and Serotonin	Roxindole
	Increases Dopamine	Parlodel, Mirapex, Amineptine, Medifoxamine
Serotonin Antidepressants	Turns On Serotonin-1A Receptors	Vilzadone, Ipsapirone, Zalospirone, GSK-163090, GSK-588045, CP-448
Norepinephrine Antidepressants	Turns Off Norepinephrine Alpha-2 Receptors	Idazoxan, Fluparoxan, Septiline, Yohimbine
	Turns On Norepinephrine Beta-3 Receptors	Amibegron
MAO Inhibitors	Increases Serotonin, Norepinephrine, Dopamine	Tyrima, Brofaromine, Pirlindole, Toloxatone, MDL-72394
Growth Hormone Antidepressants	Increases Growth Hormone, Norepinephrine, Dopamine	Valdoxan

[1] In addition to the names mentioned in the text, I have included medications that are so new that they have not yet been named. You can follow their codes through the Internet until they are given their own names.

[2] See the text for explanations of how the new antidepressants work.

Is there any way a medication could turn off stress?

We now realize that depressive individuals' overactive stress response damages and kills brain cells and helps cause depression. There are new antidepressants being developed that act directly on this excess stress response, and these "anti-stress antidepressants" are just around the corner. Currently, there are prospective antidepressants that will fight stress in several ways:

- Brain-Derived Neurotrophic Factor Antidepressants: As you know, the brain produces a chemical called brain-derived neurotrophic factor (BDNF), which heals brain cells that are damaged by depression and stress. Although current antidepressants have some effect on brain protective chemicals, these are the first antidepressants that work primarily to stop unipolar major depression by increasing BDNF. They include Rolipram, Cistamine, Semax, and others. There is also evidence that exercise, music, intellectual stimulation, some current antidepressants, mood stabilizers, and anticonvulsive medications can increase BDNF, although we still have much to learn about these effects.

- NMDA Receptor Antidepressants: Another way of blocking your body's overactive stress response is to keep it from being turned on in the first place. Namenda (generic name: memantine) is currently used for the treatment of Alzheimer's disease. Rilutek (generic name: riluzole) is now used to treat amyotrophic lateral sclerosis (ALS). Mifeprex (generic name: mifepristone) is now being used as a female hormone blocker. All of these and some new medications being developed turn off brain cell switches called NMDA receptors, which stops your body from overproducing steroid stress hormones. These medications are currently being tested for safety and efficacy as antidepressants.

- Glucocorticoid Receptor Antidepressant: At least one new antidepressant stops the production of steroid stress hormones by turning off brain cell switches called glucocorticoid-2 receptors. This action also promotes weight loss, offering the possibility of a combined antidepressant and weight loss medication.
- Corticotrophin Releasing Factor Antidepressants: Antalarmin, Pexacerfont, and other new antidepressants stop steroid stress hormones by turning off brain cell switches called corticotrophin releasing factor-1 receptors. In addition to stopping depression, they may help protect the body against anxiety, stomach ulcers, irritable bowel disease, high blood pressure, and heart disease.
- Vasopressin Receptor Antidepressant: Still another anti-stress antidepressant under development turns off the stress response by turning off brain cell switches called vasopressin-1 receptors. Pharmaceutical companies hope it will stop depression, reduce PTSD, and control excess body weight.

Is depression caused by brain inflammation that can be treated with aspirin?

Common over-the-counter drugs like aspirin will not relieve depression, but some other, new anti-inflammatory medications may. Emend (generic name: aprepitant) is currently used to reduce nausea caused by chemotherapy. Together with new drugs such as Casopitant and Orvepitant, Emend stops brain inflammation by turning off brain switches called inflammatory neurokinin-1 receptors. It is hoped that these new medications may relieve depression as well as improve asthma, arthritis, cough, inflammatory bowel disease, and pancreatitis.

What is the newest development in modern anti-depressants?

Other than MAOIs, modern antidepressants mainly stimulate one or two of the three main neurochemicals involved in depression. Triple reuptake blockers (TRIs) increase all three neurotransmitters: serotonin, norepinephrine, and dopamine. Such triple reuptake inhibitors will probably work faster and have greater effectiveness with fewer side effects than the antidepressants we have now. Several examples are listed in the table.

Are doctors testing medications used for Parkinson's disease to see if they treat depression?

We already know that medications that help increase dopamine can be effective antidepressants. For example, Wellbutrin is an antidepressant currently on the market that improves mood and energy by increasing dopamine (see Chapter 5, Newer Antidepressant Medications). Several medications that are currently being used for Parkinson's disease also increase dopamine, including Parlodel (bromocriptine) and Mirapex (pramipexole). They are now being tested to see if they can provide safe and effective treatment for unipolar major depression.

Will there be any new MAOIs?

Tyrima, brofaromine, pirlindole, toloxatone, and others drugs in development are new MAO inhibitors that pharmaceutical companies are hoping will have commercial potential. Given the current negative climate toward existing monoamine oxidase inhibitors, doctors will likely require that they work very well and are relatively free from side effects before they'll prescribe them.

I read there is a new combined sleep and anti-depressant medication coming up. What is it?

Valdoxan (generic name: agomelatine) is a new medication that increases growth hormone (melatonin), norepinephrine, and dopamine. Psychopharmacologists hope to produce a medication that banishes depression and makes it easier to fall asleep without sedatives.

Is there any medical way to cure depression without medication?

You may have heard of some exciting new medical procedures that are said to reduce depression symptoms without medications or psychotherapy. Currently these procedures are promoted for people who have severe, life-threatening depression that has not responded to any other treatment. Everyone is watching the success of these new procedures to see if they will provide a revolution in successful unipolar major depression treatment.

Can depression be eliminated with magnets?

In repetitive transcranial magnetic stimulation (rTMS), a coil of wire encased in plastic is placed on the patient's head. It is then charged with a powerful electrical current to create a series of brief, rapid, ultra-strong magnetic pulses. These pulses of magnetism reduce depression, possibly by causing serotonin, norepinephrine, and dopamine to be released in the brain. No electricity enters your body, there is no interruption of consciousness, and there is no need for anesthesia or sedation. Some people experience a slightly painful sensation on the head at the time of treatment or headaches afterward, but there is no sense of electrical stimulation.

In one study, patients who had not responded to antidepressants obtained relief from their depression after taking rTMS several times a week for four to six weeks. Continuing rTMS treatments or medications were used to keep their depression at bay after that.

While rTMS has been approved by the U.S. Food and Drug Administration for use in treatment-resistant depression, you may want to wait for more information on rTMS before you decide to run giant magnetic currents through your head.

Is there a pacemaker on the market that stops depression?

Vagus nerve stimulation (VNS) is a medical procedure that is being used to treat severe depression that has not responded to medications or psychotherapy. VNS is more invasive than rTMS; a doctor must make an incision and insert wires into your chest. These wires are wrapped around your vagus nerve, a long nerve that travels vertically through your chest. The wires are then connected to a cardiac pacemaker-like device that is implanted under your skin. After the procedure, you are left with an incision scar and a small bump on your chest. The pacemaker is programmed to provide a pulse of electrical current through your vagus nerve at predetermined intervals.

The antidepressant effect of VNS was discovered by accident. Stimulating the vagus nerve in the chest was first used to stop uncontrollable epileptic seizures. Depressed epileptics found that the VNS helped reduce both their seizures *and* their depression. The most common adverse effects of VNS are pain at the incision, hoarseness, husky voice, and shortness of breath. Some people have an uncomfortable sensation in their chest periodically throughout the day, each time their vagus nerves are stimulated.

Despite its potential usefulness, VNS has many safety issues and is currently a rather drastic procedure for the treatment of unipolar major depression. Surgically opening your chest is a serious procedure that leaves you vulnerable to infection, and we do not yet know enough about the long-term effects of VNS on your vagus nerve or your health in general.

How does convulsant therapy work for depression?

Having an epileptic seizure can stop even the most severe depression suddenly and completely, likely because seizures naturally release an immediate flood of serotonin, norepinephrine, and dopamine into the brain. Seizures also release brain-healing BDNF, which repairs stress-damaged brain cells and causes new brain cells to be born and proliferate in areas of the brain that have been damaged by unipolar major depression.

Long ago, doctors witnessed immediate and dramatic depression recoveries after their patients had seizures, and they conceived of the idea of using mild electricity to cause the smallest possible controlled seizure as a treatment for severe unipolar major depression. Every year, we see new technical developments in this technique that make older technology look prehistoric. Recently, magnetic stimulation greater than that used for rTMS has been used to cause the tiny seizure without using any electricity at all.

There are two situations that make patients consider convulsant therapy. People who are afraid of taking their lives may request convulsant therapy as the only treatment that can stop their depression and suicidality right away. Also, pregnant women who are so severely depressed that they are endangering their own lives and the lives of their babies can request convulsant therapy to put a rapid end to their depression. Most authorities agree that convulsant therapy is safer than medications for the baby because the convulsive stimulation bypasses the unborn child.

Are these alternative treatments safe?

Before jumping into any of these rather extreme solutions, make sure you have double-checked your diagnosis and confirmed that you have already exhausted simpler and safer treatment options. Then, if you still want to try these techniques, take your time and discuss the risks and benefits of these procedures with your psychiatrist, primary care physician, and the doctors who will perform the procedure. Do not be afraid to obtain several opinions and to discuss these procedures with your therapist, family members, and friends before you make a decision to either try one of these techniques or to wait until we know more and have even better options.

Chapter 8

FINDING A DOCTOR

- How can a doctor help me with my depression?
- What's the first step in treating unipolar major depression?
- Can all medical doctors treat my depression?
- How are psychiatrists different from other medical doctors?
- What are the advantages in seeing a psychiatrist over other health professionals?
- How can I find a good psychiatrist?
- What should I ask a psychiatrist before I see her?
- What should I look for in a psychiatrist?
- What if I have to wait too long to get an appointment with the psychiatrist I want to see?
- What does a psychiatrist usually do during the first appointment?
- What is the psychiatrist looking for in our first few sessions?
- What should I look for in the first appointment to indicate that a new doctor is right for me?
- Can I choose my own psychiatrist through an HMO or clinic?
- What if I am not satisfied with the treatment my current doctor is providing?
- What do I do if I feel my doctor is making all my decisions for me and not allowing me to help find the right treatment?

How can a doctor help me with my depression?

A doctor can work with you to help you find new options to relieve your depression. The best thing you can do to make your depression treatment a success is to find a doctor who will work with you and whom you can trust. The two of you need to work as a team, making decisions, sharing information, and discussing the benefits and risks of different treatment options. It should be a two-way street with mutual participation in all decisions. If you feel that you do not know enough to participate in the clinical decisions, then it is the responsibility of your physician to educate you until you do. Do not be afraid to point this out to him or her if the situation comes up.

If you already have a doctor and it does not seem possible to develop this type of working relationship and mutual trust, you may want to look for a new doctor. It's important that you get a correct diagnosis and the right treatment, and you'll need the right doctor in order to get it.

What's the first step in treating unipolar major depression?

If you have not had a physical examination in the last six months, you need to get one before you start your depression treatment. A physical examination will make sure your health is good and that you are not suffering from physical problems that will confound the treatment of your major depression. A basic physical examination includes listening to your heart and lungs, examining your liver and kidneys, performing a short neurological examination, a urine test, and taking blood for blood count, electrolytes, and a thyroid-screening test. Some psychiatrists will do this examination themselves, but if you have a regular internist or family doctor, you may prefer to go to him.

Can all medical doctors treat my depression?

All licensed medical doctors can legally treat unipolar major depression if they choose to do so. All physicians learned about depression in medical school as part of their general medical training. The differences in doctors' ability to treat depression lies in the training and experience they had after medical school. There are several types of doctors who regularly treat depression, and it is a good idea to understand the differences between them.

Physicians who provide primary care, including general practitioners, internists, family doctors, and obstetricians/gynecologists, may prescribe sedatives and antidepressants and/or refer depressed patients to psychiatrists and other mental health professionals. If they choose to treat depression, most primary care doctors have experience with one or two antidepressants that they use for all or most of their patients. Primary care physicians are often less rigorous in their diagnosis of depression than psychiatrists are.

If you want your primary care physician to treat your depression, it is still a good idea to have a consultation with a psychiatrist, to get the benefits of her expertise in diagnosis and treatment planning.

How are psychiatrists different from other medical doctors?

Psychiatrists have graduated medical school and a practical medical internship and are licensed to practice any type of medicine. In addition, psychiatrists complete three more years of additional training in an accredited psychiatry program. Psychiatrists receive extensive specialized education, training, and clinical experience in diagnosing unipolar major depression and in the pharmacology of medications used to treat it. Because of their specialty training, psychiatrists may be more expensive and may be in short supply in some geographic areas.

What are the advantages in seeing a psychiatrist over other health professionals?

In most cases, psychiatrists offer the very best treatment for unipolar major depression. Compared with other professionals, they usually have the most experience treating patients with severe depression. In addition to their understanding of the wealth of medications used to treat unipolar major depression, psychiatrists are the only medical doctors who are fully trained in psychotherapy for depression.

Psychiatrists can tell you for sure if you have unipolar major depression, and they can offer a wide range of different types of treatments to find the best match for you. They should be able to discuss all the relevant benefits, side effects, and risks of whatever treatment you choose. They may offer to do both medications and psychotherapy together in the same session.

How can I find a good psychiatrist?

The best first step is to ask your primary care doctor if he knows a psychiatrist in the community that he has worked with and respects. If any of your friends go to psychiatrists, ask your friends whether they would recommend their doctors to you. Look on the Internet for the nearest local and state branches of the American Medical Association or the American Psychiatric Association, and find out if they give referrals to psychiatrists in your area. Good psychiatrists often, but not always, belong to one or both of these professional organizations. Search the Internet for the websites of psychiatrists in your area; you can often tell a lot about someone from their website. If there is a university hospital or medical school nearby, call the psychiatry department and ask if there are psychiatrists in the community to whom they refer patients.

What should I ask a psychiatrist before I see her?

You want to find a psychiatrist with good training and successful experience treating depressed patients. To find out about her training, call the prospective psychiatrist and ask when and where she went to medical school and where she did her psychiatry residency training. You should not go to a "psychiatrist" who has not completed residency training in psychiatry. You need a doctor with the right training to help guide your treatment.

To find out about their experience, ask the psychiatrist how long she has been in practice. Ask if she usually treats unipolar major depression with medications or therapy and what proportion of her current patients are being treated for unipolar major depression.

While on the telephone, pay attention to your initial impression of the doctor. Does she sound personal, friendly, and caring, or distant, rushed, and irritated? You can form a first impression in a few moments over the telephone. It's important you find a psychiatrist with whom you feel completely comfortable and who will get to know you well enough to help you determine the correct course of your treatment.

You can also ask psychiatrists or their office staff how much time you will have with the doctor during the evaluation appointment and each follow-up visit. Ask specifically how much the psychiatrist charges for your evaluation appointment and subsequent office visits, because they are often priced differently. You should be prepared to pay for the initial appointment even if you do not continue seeing the doctor. Ask how frequently the psychiatrist usually sees her depressed patients. Between once a week and once a month is a common frequency when starting unipolar major depression treatment.

This may seem like too many questions, but you can ask them in just a few moments, and after the first few questions, the psychiatrist may begin to volunteer information without being asked. If you have a good feeling about her, then make an appointment for an evaluation. This is where the psychiatrist examines and talks to you, decides on a diagnosis, and discusses treatment.

What should I look for in a psychiatrist?

A good track record is the most important thing to consider in choosing a psychiatrist. If a psychiatrist has consistently helped his patients feel better, then you probably want him to be your doctor. Your psychiatrist should have plenty of clinical experience. This can only be obtained by evaluating and successfully treating many other patients like you who suffer from unipolar major depression. Your psychiatrist must be a skilled diagnostician to make sure you get the right diagnosis. He must be able to give you a detailed evaluation and be able to apply the official diagnostic criteria for depression (see Appendix B). You do not want a psychiatrist who diagnoses by first impressions or instinct, because these diagnoses are often wrong. Your psychiatrist should be a good pharmacologist who keeps up with the current medical literature and can offer you a choice of the most up-to-date medications for unipolar major depression. He needs to know more than what is in the textbooks. Whether or not you ask your psychiatrist to provide you with psychotherapy, he must be an accomplished psychotherapist in order to understand your psychological makeup, to maintain effective communication, and to help you make the best of your medications. Your psychiatrist should be a good physician and healer in the broadest sense of the word. In the depths of your depression, he must be a source of understanding, help, reassurance, and inspiration. Your psychiatrist must be a good person and a good role model for you. The strength of his personality may be the only thing helping you to stay alive during the tough period before medications and psychotherapy start working.

What if I have to wait too long to get an appointment with the psychiatrist I want to see?

If the doctor has a busy schedule, you may have to wait weeks for an appointment. If you want to get in to see the doctor sooner, let her know that you would like to be called if there's a late cancellation. If you do this, be prepared to make yourself available at the last moment.

If you cannot get an appointment with the psychiatrist you choose or you cannot get one soon enough, ask for a referral from your primary care doctor to the psychiatrist you want to get in and see. Referrals usually get a faster and more positive response than calling up the psychiatrist's office yourself. If your primary care doctor will not refer you, ask other doctors that you or your family know. If you know any of the psychiatrist's patients, it is fair to ask them if they would call up and ask if the psychiatrist will see you on their recommendation.

What does a psychiatrist usually do during the first appointment?

The first appointment procedure differs from doctor to doctor, but here's a very general rundown of what you might expect from a good evaluation. Many psychiatrists will ask you to complete paperwork before the appointment, which may include filling out psychological tests and scales. Then expect to spend twenty to fifty minutes with the doctor telling him about yourself, your depression, and what led up to it. The psychiatrist will probably ask you some follow-up questions and then give you his diagnostic impression. Ideally, you'll discuss the various treatment options that the doctor thinks might be useful for you, including their benefits and risks. If you both agree on a treatment plan, you'll likely leave the office with a prescription and/or an agreement to do psychotherapy. If you need more time to come up with a mutually satisfactory plan, you'll schedule another appointment.

In the first few sessions, it's a good idea to make a list of the ways that your depression is keeping you from getting what you want in your life. During subsequent meetings, you can discuss your progress and improve the treatment.

What is the psychiatrist looking for in our first few sessions?

Your doctor needs to understand who you are and interact with you in person to assess your degree of happiness and sadness, hopefulness and discouragement, comfort and anxiety, confidence and fear, fulfillment and loneliness, and calmness and agitation. Your psychiatrist gathers this information from observing your expressions, appearance, speech, tone of voice, posture, body language, and gestures as the two of you talk together. At the same time, she is evaluating your mental functions like attention, memory, ability to follow logic, and your ability to make abstract analyses.

After you have begun treatment, your psychiatrist may measure your progress using clinical scales and tests to keep track of your symptoms and improvement in work, school, family, and social relationships. The doctor needs to see you to compare the way you seem now with her memory and notes on how you were in the past. This will help her assess how well you are healing from unipolar major depression and whether anything important is missing from your treatment.

What should I look for in the first appointment to indicate that a new doctor is right for me?

Be sure that the new doctor is willing to answer your questions and to explain his opinions until you thoroughly understand them. Communication is one of the most important parts of successful psychiatric treatment, and you need a doctor who speaks clearly and uses language that you can understand. You do not want a doctor who shares a lot of personal information or tells you about his own problems. You made your appointment so that the doctor can help you, not the other way around.

You should never continue to see any doctor who says or does anything improper, unprofessional, or in poor taste. There is no room for this in the practice of modern medicine. On the other hand, do not worry if the doctor is not smiley, bubbly, or upbeat, or doesn't tell you that everything is great and that you are wonderful. You are there to work on a serious problem, not to get vacuous reassurance. Do not be put off if the doctor briefly answers a page or telephone call during your session. The doctor is responsible for other patients who might be having life-threatening emergencies. You will appreciate this if you ever need to call your doctor with your own emergency.

Most of all, see how you feel while you are together with the new psychiatrist. If you feel comfortable in his presence, it is a sign that this doctor may be the one for you.

Can I choose my own psychiatrist through an HMO or clinic?

Many insurance organizations will give you a list of several doctors to choose from, whereas HMOs and both private and public clinics may want to pick a doctor for you. If so, this doctor may be willing to refer you to a psychiatrist if you wish. And if you do not like the doctor to whom you are assigned, you can usually make a change. In any case, if you want a certain doctor or one with certain training and experience, make this clear early in the selection process so that you have a better chance of getting what you want.

Do not be concerned if you are assigned to a doctor who works in a clinic or has an unimpressive office. There are wonderful doctors everywhere, no matter where they work or how much money they charge.

What if I am not satisfied with the treatment my current doctor is providing?

If you are not sure about your treatment, the first step is to discuss it frankly with your current doctor. In a good working relationship, it should be possible for either of you to speak your mind in a positive, constructive way. Tell your current doctor you are not satisfied, and ask what she can suggest. Do not be alarmed if she wants time to think about it and consult her own resources; you want the benefit of her best judgment.

If this does not fix things, the next step is to obtain a second opinion. Second opinions can be very useful, and your current doctor should value a helpful new viewpoint. It is perfectly appropriate for you to ask your current doctor to suggest or call a specialist to get you a second opinion. If you do not want to involve your current doctor, you can find a psychiatric consultant and make an appointment on your own. When you meet with the new psychiatrist, make sure you tell him honestly about your current treatment and make it clear you're looking for a second opinion on it. If you are considering replacing your current doctor, be up-front with the new doctor, and ask if he thinks it's merited.

What do I do if I feel my doctor is making all my decisions for me and not allowing me to help find the right treatment?

Doctors vary in their attitude according to their age, type of training, personality, and personal hang-ups. In the past, many doctors were encouraged to take the role of a parent who does your thinking for you, rather than making sure you're an equal team member. Some doctors you meet just may not be very good at working together with their patients. If you're feeling left out of treatment decisions, or if you feel that your current course isn't the best one for you, discuss this with your current doctor. If this doesn't work, begin looking for a new one.

Chapter 9

SEEKING THERAPY

- What is psychotherapy?
- What are the advantages of psychotherapy?
- Is psychotherapy as effective as medications?
- What can psychotherapy give me that I cannot get from my medication?
- Should I choose psychotherapy or medication treatment for my depression?
- Should I start medicine or therapy first?
- Why do I have to pay a psychotherapist when I can talk to friends and family?
- Are psychiatrists trained to do psychotherapy?
- I thought that depression is emotional—why is my thinking so disturbed?
- Why are my thoughts all so negative?
- What types of psychotherapy are available to treat my depression?
- How can I find a good psychotherapist?
- What questions should I ask a psychotherapist?
- What is the most important thing in choosing a psychotherapist?
- Can I ask my psychiatrist to be my therapist?
- Can I pick my own psychotherapist if I go to an HMO or clinic for my mental health care?

What is psychotherapy?

Psychotherapy is the name given to a large group of techniques that seek to change what happens inside your mind from outside, usually but not always through talking. According to the Mayo Clinic, psychotherapy "is a general term for a process of treating mental and emotional disorders by talking about your condition and related issues with a mental health provider." Basically, psychotherapy helps people discuss and learn about their disorders in order to combat them.

What are the advantages of psychotherapy?

Psychotherapy can help you recover from depression, correct negative distortions, break bad habits, and generally get your life back on track, with few side effects. No matter what you might have heard about psychotherapy before, bad or good, it can be an excellent and important treatment for unipolar major depression. Unfortunately, psychotherapy is woefully underused in this country. In one survey, only 25 percent of people with unipolar major depression were ever encouraged to try psychotherapy.

Is psychotherapy as effective as medications?

Psychotherapy works better for some people, and medications work better for other people. The two approaches work differently and complement each other—there's absolutely no reason not to do both together and enjoy the benefits of both.

What can psychotherapy give me that I cannot get from my medication?

You cannot talk to a pill. Meeting with a psychotherapist can be a warm, personal, and fulfilling experience. Psychotherapy provides you with tools to learn about yourself and to control your moods, thoughts, and personal mental health. It can help you eliminate the habits of thought and behavior that make you more vulnerable to depression. In addition, psychotherapy can help you plan and achieve your life goals, improve your personal relationships, organize your free time, and help you recover from the mess that is often left after depression is healed.

In contrast, psychotherapy cannot reach into the cells of your brain and adjust them so they work normally and naturally again. It cannot directly heal brain cell damage or protect your brain from future damage. It cannot directly improve your brain's ability to pay attention, to organize thoughts, or to make abstract and logical conclusions. For patients who are too withdrawn and depressed or too cognitively impaired to participate in psychotherapy, medication may be the only option until depression has begun to heal.

Should I choose psychotherapy or medication treatment for my depression?

Who says you have to choose? For years, reliable research has shown that the best treatment for unipolar major depression is a combination of psychotherapy *and* medication. People who combine psychotherapy with medications usually get better results than those who try to struggle through with either one alone.

Should I start medicine or therapy first?

If the process of depression has affected your ability to pay attention, follow logic, and/or perform abstract thinking, it will make it difficult for you to participate in your psychotherapy. In this case, starting medications first can improve your cognition so you can participate in your psychotherapy more effectively and make faster, better progress in your treatment.

Why do I have to pay a psychotherapist when I can talk to friends and family?

In the first place, you *should* take the opportunity to get support from your trusted family members and friends. They can listen to your thoughts and feelings, demonstrate their care for you, and show you that you're not alone with your depression.

However, a professional psychotherapist offers much more than talking with family members and friends. Psychotherapeutic techniques have been developed and improved for more than one hundred years specifically to help individuals with depression like yours. Ideally, your psychotherapist will be trained in one or more types of psychotherapy that target unipolar major depression and relieve depressive symptoms most effectively.

An experienced psychotherapist will have already helped many other people like you get over their depression. They usually know when to listen and what to say to help you. Furthermore, psychotherapy can help you create a buffer against stressful events. By reducing the effects of life stresses, psychotherapy can help decrease the levels of stress neurochemicals in your brain and make it easier to recover from your depression.

Are psychiatrists trained to do psychotherapy?

All psychiatrists are trained as psychotherapists. Many psychiatrists prefer to provide both medications and therapy, while others prefer to focus on just one type of treatment. When you see the term "doctor and therapist" in this book, you will know that it can be one person providing both.

I thought that depression is emotional—why is my thinking so disturbed?

Most people who are naive about depression think that it is only about having negative emotions like sadness, anger, anxiety, and loneliness. Depressed individuals soon learn that abnormal thoughts are actually the heart of their depression and the source of most of its problems. Thoughts of worthlessness drive emotions of guilt and remorse. Nihilistic thoughts of hopelessness and death cause emotions of desperation and doom that can hijack your future plans and may even threaten your survival. Problems with thinking and decision making can also cause failures in your work, school, and personal life, producing even more negative emotions.

On the bright side, your thoughts provide you with tools to fight your unipolar major depression. Most of psychotherapy consists of changing your emotions by changing the way that you think.

Why are my thoughts all so negative?

Unipolar major depression causes negative thoughts to intrude into your consciousness and stay there, repeating endlessly. It is like the gate to your conscious mind is broken, so that unwanted bad thoughts come into your mind and drive out your more desirable positive thoughts. As this process continues, the strongest, most negative guilty, hopeless, and miserable thoughts take possession of your mind, and your depression experience worsens. Psychotherapy can help you become more aware of these unnatural thought processes and help you find ways to break the intrusive thought cycle.

This intensification of negative thoughts also facilitates the development of fantasies that become darker and more distorted as depression worsens. They cause you to imagine that things in your life are worse than they are, that you have bad luck, that you are doomed, that nothing can ever get better, and that anything you do will lead to loss and sorrow. Because of this distortion, you may think that everything you tried in the past was a failure. You may develop the unfounded fantasy that you will never be able to do anything right. Your problems appear larger than they are, and you fantasize that they are impossible to solve and intolerable to live with. During strong episodes of depression, you believe these fantasies are real. Psychotherapy can help you challenge these distorted fantasies and return to a more normal, natural, objective view of yourself and your life.

Fortunately, psychotherapy can help you gain control over your thoughts and help you see through the artificial distortions you may have come to accept.

What types of psychotherapy are available to treat my depression?

The following is a list of different types of psychotherapy that you may encounter.

- Psychoeducation: Psychoeducation (PE) is the process of learning about unipolar major depression, what causes it, and what makes it go away. Your doctor and therapist should contribute actively to PE to help you understand your thoughts, emotions, and behaviors, and the ways to make things better. PE can help you learn how to live a healthy life, reduce stress, and minimize your vulnerability to having another depressive episode. Many studies show that PE works as well or better than other types of psychotherapy for relieving depression. And in fact, this book was written to help you understand your depression, and the act of reading it already makes you a participant in psychoeducation. You will find other ways to extend your depression education in Appendix A, Resources.

You should make sure that your doctor and therapist know that you want to share their knowledge about unipolar major depression and its treatment. They should discuss the benefits and risks of all your health choices with you until you feel comfortable making treatment decisions. This psychoeducation is an essential part of depression treatment, and in many cases, it is required by law.

- Behavioral Therapy: Behavioral therapy (BT) uses learning, training, and behavioral techniques that were specifically developed to reduce depression. BT teaches relaxation techniques that can protect you against stress and the depression it causes. It helps you plan activities that you enjoy, and it helps you become a participant in your life again. BT can change the negative workings of your mind by helping you remember prior, undepressed ways of thinking, feeling, and acting.

  You can find relaxation exercises in Chapter 13, Stress-Reduction Techniques, and behavioral therapy programs on pages 246–250 for you to do at home. BT requires homework, but depressed people seem to be able to complete it relatively easily. Unfortunately, only a limited number of psychotherapists are trained in behavioral therapy, and they may be difficult to find.

- Cognitive Therapy: Cognitive therapy (CT) was developed specifically for the treatment of depression. CT is based on the notion that we develop basic patterns of thinking, like overgeneralization, negative filtering, catastrophic thinking, and attempts to predict the future, that need to be changed in order to recover from unipolar major depression patterns. CT also aims to correct erroneous core beliefs that stem from depression, such as feelings that you are bad, weak, helpless, unworthy, or unlovable. Studies have shown that CT is useful for the treatment of depression.

Unfortunately, some severely depressed individuals are not able to do the homework that is required in CT, especially if they do not have energy or free time. It can also be difficult to find qualified cognitive psychotherapists in many locations, but the CT crowd is growing.

- Psychodynamic Psychotherapy: Psychodynamic psychotherapy (PP) is an outgrowth of Freudian and Jungian psychoanalysis that helps you acquire insight into your inner self and use it as a tool to resolve your depression. Over time, you may have developed bad habits and maladaptive ways of dealing with your depression by pretending your problems do not exist (denial), running away from them (withdrawal), pretending someone else is responsible for them (projection), or expressing your frustration through annoying others (passive aggression). If any of these sound familiar, then PP may be the answer.

  Modern psychodynamic psychotherapy uses the interaction between psychotherapist and client as a tool to reveal internal assumptions and fantasies. It is potentially very helpful for unipolar major depression. Although this approach is thought to be slow, many PP therapists are trained in brief psychodynamic therapies specifically targeted at unipolar major depression.

- Interpersonal Therapy: Interpersonal therapy (IPT) is a brief psychotherapy specifically developed for the treatment of unipolar major depression. IPT examines significant relationships in your life and helps control your depression by improving communication and gaining insight. Improving your understanding of important relationships, social interactions, and communications can improve your life dramatically.

- Group Therapy: Group therapy provides a safe environment to share thoughts and feelings with others who also suffer from unipolar major depression. It is an opportunity to acquire insight from other peoples' experiences and to hear about new coping strategies that others have discovered. Group psychotherapists may be trained in interpersonal, psychodynamic, family, supportive, or other types of psychotherapy, and could use any or all of them in their groups. The quality of group therapy depends very much on the training and expertise of the professional psychotherapist who leads the group. Group therapy that is just a bunch of unsupervised chatting will not help your depression. Similarly, groups that have broken away from a professional psychotherapist and simply meet on their own, as well as groups led by untrained leaders or other patients, can also be more damaging than helpful. These waste your valuable time and money, and whether they make your depression better or worse is just a toss-up.

- Family Therapy: Family therapy (FT) brings your spouse, parents, and children into your therapy session. It places emphasis on communication and problem solving between individuals in the session. Problems identified in one member of the family are examined in the context of the family system and the contributions of its members. Family therapy is popular but may be more useful for problems that arise from dysfunction in the family than for problems that arise from lack of control over thoughts and emotions (depression).

- Supportive Therapy: Supportive therapy (ST) is positive social feedback developed into a form of psychotherapy. ST seeks to encourage, nurture, and reassure you that things are not as bad as you think, that you will be successful, and that tomorrow is another day. Unfortunately, from the depths of depression, this rosy view is often annoying, and it can be disconcerting to be feeling so bad at the same time your psychotherapist acts as if the world is her oyster.

Some supportive therapists believe that bringing back and reexperiencing past miseries and failures will cleanse them from your system. Unfortunately, this practice can make depression worse.

Overall, therapies for depression that focus on practical life changes seem to be the best way to treat unipolar major depression; ST can make you feel good for a while, but it might not help you make the changes that you need in your life.

How can I find a good psychotherapist?

Start by asking your doctor if she knows of a psychotherapist that she can confidently recommend to you. Ask your friends how they like their own psychotherapists. Go to local meetings of mental health organizations, listen to what others say about their own psychotherapists, and watch psychotherapists from your community giving presentations. Visit the websites of psychotherapists practicing near you. See Appendix A, Resources, for more leads.

What questions should I ask a psychotherapist?

Before or during the first appointment, ask your potential psychotherapist about his licensure, where he obtained his postgraduate psychotherapy training, and how long he has been in practice. Ask what type of psychotherapy he was trained in—if he cannot tell you, then this is a bad sign. If the potential psychotherapist is still in training, contact his supervisor and ask her the same questions. Because some types of therapy are more specifically tailored for depression than others, the type of psychotherapy that your potential psychotherapist uses is a major concern, and the amount of experience and success he has had using this type of psychotherapy is especially important.

Also ask about fees; these can range widely among different therapists.

What is the most important thing in choosing a psychotherapist?

After you have found a potential psychotherapist, you must see how you feel when you are sitting in the room with her. If you are comfortable and feel some trust for the person sitting across from you, then the two of you may have the makings of a good professional therapeutic team.

Can I ask my psychiatrist to be my therapist?

Sure—every psychiatrist is trained and experienced in psychotherapy. Some prefer to provide medications, some offer medications and psychotherapy, and many psychiatrists are solely psychotherapists. Your current psychiatrist will be happy to tell you what she can offer you.

She may already understand you and your depression, and you may already have formed a good working relationship with her that will help your therapy. On the other hand, if you prefer a psychotherapist that has a different style or personality than your psychiatrist, you may want to look elsewhere.

Can I pick my own psychotherapist if I go to an HMO or clinic for my mental health care?

It depends on where you go. Most HMOs and clinics are used to making these decisions for you, although you still may be able to make a change if you have a problem. If you have a preference for a certain person, psychotherapy style, or medical background, or want a psychotherapist of a particular gender, age, or ethnicity, make your preferences known early in the selection process in order to have the best chance of getting what you want.

Here is something to remember: Quality in psychotherapy depends on the individual psychotherapist, not the location of her office or how much she charges.

Chapter 10

CHOOSING BETWEEN PSYCHO- THERAPISTS

- What are the differences between types of mental health workers?
- Who is the most affordable: a psychiatrist, a professional psychologist, a social worker, or a counselor?
- Can psychologists, counselors, or social workers prescribe antidepressants?
- Does hypnosis work well for unipolar major depression?
- Are holistic approaches like therapeutic touch effective in treating depression?
- What are the roles of religion and prayer?
- Should I get a religious practitioner who is also trained as a counselor?
- What is "Internet psychotherapy?"
- Can a person practice psychotherapy without any training?
- With whom can I talk about my grief after losing a loved one?
- Will grief go away on its own?
- What should I do if my grief and depression are making me think of suicide?

What are the differences between types of mental health workers?

There can be many people involved in your recovery from a depressed episode—here are some of the people who can help and the different areas they are trained in.

- Psychiatrists: Psychiatrists go to school for at least twelve years. They go to four years of college, four years of medical school to earn an MD doctoral degree, one year of hospital internship, and three additional years of training in psychiatry in an accredited program. Afterward, they may elect to take on an additional one to three more years of training as a university fellow or subspecialist. Psychiatrists learn the biology of emotional illness, the function of the brain, medications and how to use them, and how to perform psychotherapy. Because of this extensive training, psychiatrists often charge higher fees than nonmedical psychotherapists in the same community.

- Professional Psychologists: Professional psychologists earn a PhD doctoral degree in a four-year graduate program and complete one year of practical internship. They may be the only sources for behavioral or cognitive psychotherapy in your community. Professional psychologists do not receive extensive training in the biology or pharmacology of depression in the brain and nervous system. Professional psychologists' fees are usually less than psychiatrists' fees and more than counselors' fees.

- Mental Health Nurses: Mental health nurses complete either a two- or three-year basic nursing program and choose to earn extra certification in mental health nursing. Many nurses have considerable experience and wisdom, especially about treating depression in the hospital.

- Social Workers: Social workers receive a master's degree in social work (MSW) and are specially trained in the case management of moderate and severe mental illness, particularly within the context of public health. They are usually knowledgeable about federal, state, and local services that can help depressed individuals and their families. They are often trained in family psychotherapy. Licensed clinical social workers (LCSWs) have extra training in psychotherapy and mental illness. Some social workers provide service at low or deferred cost.
- Marriage and Family Counselors: Marriage and family counselors' roles and licensure vary between states. They usually complete a two-year master's degree (MA). They are often trained in family psychotherapy or supportive psychotherapy. Counselors usually receive little training in the diagnosis of unipolar major depression and no training in the biology of depression. Family counselors' fees are usually lower than the fees charged by psychiatrists and professional psychologists.

Who is the most affordable: a psychiatrist, a professional psychologist, a social worker, or a counselor?

People rack their brains over this one. Would it be cheaper to see a psychiatrist who would provide both medications and therapy at the same price? Are counselors and social workers a better choice because they (usually) charge less than psychiatrists and professional psychologists? Is it better to find the cheapest psychotherapist available (usually a student in counseling or social work)?

Fortunately, there is a simple answer to this thorny problem: Whatever arrangement keeps you the most healthy and free from depression is the best and cheapest solution in the end. If you get poor treatment, you will need extra appointments, second opinions, or hospitalization, and these costs mount up. Severe illness can deplete your savings, create problems at work, disturb your family, and wreck your social life. Every recurrent episode of depression can make the disorder more severe and less treatable. Remember, price is not always synonymous with quality. Find a doctor and therapist whom you can trust and with whom you feel comfortable. The way to save money is to get the best treatment for you.

Can psychologists, counselors, or social workers prescribe antidepressants?

In most states, only medical doctors can prescribe medications. A few states have given doctoral psychologists the ability to prescribe a few drugs, but they do not receive the extensive training in human biology and psychopharmacology that is provided to medical doctors. To make sure you get a correct diagnosis and both medication *and* psychotherapy options, consult a psychiatrist.

Does hypnosis work well for unipolar major depression?

Although hypnosis can be a very effective form of therapy, it's best suited for problems like smoking, weight gain, or fear of flying. You're likely better off choosing a type of psychotherapy that has a proven track record for relieving unipolar major depression.

Are holistic approaches like therapeutic touch effective in treating depression?

In the right hands, therapeutic touch can relieve patients' anxiety, reduce chronic pain, and help patients control their fears about upcoming surgical procedures. Many holistic practitioners charge low fees, are nonthreatening, and help relieve surgeons and medical doctors of the need to provide constant reassurance to their overanxious patients. It is fine if you choose to see a holistic practitioner in addition to your accredited psychotherapist, but it's not advisable to use alternative approaches as a substitute for psychotherapies that have been proven to reduce depression.

What are the roles of religion and prayer?

An active spiritual life can be important to one's health, and your chances of beating depression can be greater if you are engaged in spiritual activity. Prayer has a long history of helping individuals get through painful and unbearable conditions. However, you still need psychotherapy and medications to handle your psychological and physical needs.

Should I get a religious practitioner who is also trained as a counselor?

While you may find this helpful if you are a religious person, it's more important that you find the best psychotherapist available in your area. When you explore psychotherapy, you want a therapist who is well educated, experienced, and has a good track record for relieving unipolar major depression. If your religious counselor is the best psychotherapist available, you should definitely try her. Otherwise, keep looking for the best psychotherapist you can find, and if you want to, you can also talk to your religious counselor.

What is "Internet psychotherapy?"

"Internet psychotherapy" may refer to occasional email or texting sessions between you and your psychotherapist, usually only if one of you is out of town or cannot come to the office. Attempting to do therapy by email or texting is a poor substitute for meeting in person; you may consider it if you're out of town and are having a crisis, but it is definitely not a replacement for traditional face-to-face therapy.

You may also hear about "computer-driven psychotherapy." This is not a new idea—ever since computers started to use transistors, programmers have been trying to write computer programs that would replace a trained psychotherapist. These programs are usually a joke. Do not waste your time.

Can a person practice psychotherapy without any training?

Unfortunately, in most states, anyone can put up a sign and call himself a psychotherapist. Other fancy names like mind/body facilitator, mental health coach, treatment specialist, etc., may be made up or based on a certificate received from a questionable program. You can visit your state's website and find out if people calling themselves psychotherapists are licensed or not.

With whom can I talk about my grief after losing a loved one?

You may need to see a doctor or psychotherapist to recover from the loss of a loved one. Friends and relatives can provide you with valuable opportunities to talk about your thoughts and feelings, and you should consider accepting their offers of help. Sharing your traumatic experiences with other people can help mitigate your pain and speed your recovery from grief. At the same time, you are also aiding your helpers to cope with their grief by talking with you.

However, if support is not available or not helpful enough, it is time to engage a psychotherapist who can help you become yourself again and get back in the swing of normal life. Remember, the loved one you have lost would not like you to undergo pain and suffering because of his or her passing.

Here is a caveat: Some psychotherapists do not have experience with successful grief therapy. For example, some inexperienced therapists may marginalize your suffering by their inappropriate cheeriness and optimism. Others feel that experiencing severe pain after a loss is somehow necessary and will do little to help you alleviate it. You want an experienced therapist who can identify with and understand your bereavement and help you travel down the natural pathway to recovery.

Will grief go away on its own?

Bereavement after the loss of a loved one is an emotional reaction that can happen to anyone. Usually it gets better in a matter of months. If it does not seem to be going away or you do not want to wait, find a licensed psychotherapist experienced in grief counseling. There is no point in suffering unnecessarily.

What should I do if my grief and depression are making me think of suicide?

It is time to take aggressive action. The first thing to do is to see a psychiatrist to find out if you have developed unipolar major depression on top of your grief. If so, you need appropriate psychotherapy and medication in order for this depression to go away expediently. It is a misguided and sometimes fatal mistake to wait and wait for severe sadness to go away on its own when the real problem is a treatable episode of unipolar major depression. If your major depression has been triggered by the stress of your loss, it may go away quickly with medication or appropriate psychotherapy treatment. Then you can face any remaining grief and pass through this traumatic period naturally.

Chapter 11

TREATING DEPRESSION AT HOME

What can I do at home to help stop my depression?

Psychotherapy is an important treatment for your depression, but at the same time, there is much that you can do on your own to help speed your recovery from depression. Following are some programs inspired by behavioral psychotherapy that you can use on your own to help get your depression under control. If you are in psychotherapy, use these techniques and bring them into your therapy sessions to show your psychotherapist. If you have not yet found your psychotherapist, you can use the following techniques while you are looking for one.

What is the best thing I can do on my own to get my depression under control?

The Pleasant Events Program (PEP) is a great way to start yourself down the road to recovery. PEP helps you get back into a routine of doing things that you like, using pleasant activities to counter periods of depression. Ultimately, this will help you remember how you felt before you were depressed and rechannel your negative thoughts into positive actions.

Severe unipolar major depression makes it physically harder to get up and out of the house. Depression makes you feel that you would not like any activity you can think of doing. Nevertheless, activity will speed your recovery from depression. PEP will help you do the activities that will make you feel better.

To use PEP, carefully remove the Pleasant Events Program worksheet from the book (page 246) and make copies. Then look at all the activities listed on the left, and check the ones you like to do or used to like to do. There are extra lines on the worksheet for you to write in other things you enjoy. For each item you check, plan a time now or in the near future to do that activity, and write the planned date in the appropriate space on the program worksheet.

Every time you complete your scheduled event, circle the date to provide a record of your successful use of PEP. Every Sunday, look at your worksheet from the previous week. If you have planned a number of events and you have completed them, then you are using PEP successfully. Save your old worksheets, and review them often as tangible proof of your successful fight against depression. As you use PEP, feel free to increase your favorite activities and take out activities you do not care for. Remember that these activities are supposed to be fun; washing the dishes, painting the house, or other activities that are like work do not count.

How do I know if PEP is working for my depression?

As you continue doing the program, you should notice that you enjoy yourself more than you expected to during your activities. As you feel better and better, you will start looking forward to planning and participating in more of these enjoyable activities. Some of the activities you plan will not work out perfectly, and some will not be as fun as they could be, and that's okay. Just continue working to improve your own health, and PEP will help you fight off your depression.

Won't I just depress my friends if I hang around with them?

It's a common belief among depressed individuals that they should avoid others for fear of depressing them. This belief appears to make perfect sense when you are depressed, and it plays into distorted depressive beliefs that you are undesirable and only cause problems for others. However, unipolar major depression cannot be transmitted by proximity or contact like the measles or the flu. If you ask them, your friends and family will almost always tell you how much they look forward to spending time with you.

My life seems to be drifting away from me—what can I do on my own to hold on?

When you are depressed, you begin to withdraw from the familiar framework of your life into the world inside your mind. You forget to notice the pleasant things you see and do, the events that measure your days and help remind you that you are alive and vital. You get out of the habit of interacting with the world around you, and you forget to reap the rewards of living. The Life Activation Framework (LAF) is designed to counter these withdrawal tendencies and help you put yourself together again.

Unipolar major depression distorts your perception so that you only notice the dark, ugly, depressing things in your life. LAF provides a framework to help you notice the delightful and happy aspects of life again. It helps you enjoy and respond to the good and positive ingredients of your world and take an active role in the details of your personal life. Maybe most important, it can help you remember who you are without depression.

To use LAF, carefully remove the Life Activation Framework worksheet from the book (page 248), and make copies. Every evening for the rest of the week, sit down, look through the LAF worksheet, and check the boxes that apply to you that day. Make sure you are carefully observing everything that happens each day so that you can fill in the worksheet accurately. On Sunday, sit down with the LAF worksheet and go over the events of your life in the prior week. If you think of new items to add to the list, write them in the blank spaces on the worksheets to use next time. Save your old worksheets, and review them periodically to reinforce your progress.

You will know that LAF is working for you when you find yourself participating more and more actively in the fabric of your life and looking forward to positive experiences every day.

What can I do if I'm not sure how I feel?

The Emotion Checklist (EC) can help you pinpoint exactly how you feel. EC provides names for feelings like happiness, sadness, anxiety, and anger, listed from weak to strong in each group, and helps you analyze those emotions in the moment. This way, you can follow the changes in your emotions through the days and weeks as you emerge from your depression.

You can also use EC to help explain how you have been feeling to your doctor and therapist. If you take these sheets to your appointments, they will provide material that you can discuss as part of your ongoing treatment. As you progress, it can also show you which of your emotions are responding to therapy and which aren't.

To use EC, carefully remove the Emotion Checklist worksheet from the book (page 250) and make copies. Every few days, go through a new EC worksheet in the evening and check the words that best describe how you feel. Make a few notes to remind you what happened that day. If you are experiencing important events, you may want to fill out an EC worksheet every day. Keep your checklists, and compare them every Sunday.

EC will help you develop a rich vocabulary of words to explain your emotions. If you are not sure what emotions you are feeling, bring your EC to your next appointment, and ask your doctor and therapist to help you learn how to better identify and understand your emotions.

Chapter 12

GOOD HEALTH HABITS

- Can exercise help my depression?
- Is depression affecting my sleep?
- Are my repetitive thoughts keeping me awake?
- What is "sleep hygiene?"
- What do I do if it feels like my body simply doesn't want to sleep?
- What medications can safely help me sleep?
- How does my diet affect my depression?
- What are some good, basic dietary rules?
- Can vitamins help my depression?
- Should I take something to give me more energy?
- Are herbal supplements effective?
- Is it safe to buy supplements from the Internet?
- Are drug companies suppressing natural products to make more money from their drugs?
- What are some commonly used products that are bad for my depression?
- What about marijuana? It makes me feel less depressed after I smoke it.

Can exercise help my depression?

Numerous studies show that exercise can produce a modest reduction in depressive symptoms. There is also exciting, recent evidence that supports the idea that exercise can increase the production of brain-derived neurotrophic factor (BDNF) that repairs brain cells damaged by stress, helps produce new brain cells to replace dead ones, and protects cells from further stress. This is also one of the important ways that antidepressants block depression.

More medical doctors are getting the word every day. The English Mental Health Foundation found that more than 60 percent of English doctors now believe that controlled exercise is an effective part of unipolar major depression treatment, and 22 percent prescribe it to their depressed patients. If you do not have an exercise routine now, be prepared to create one.

Check first with your primary care doctor to find out how much and what kind of exercise is right for you. If you have no restrictions, try starting with ten to fifteen minutes of exercise daily. This could be brisk walking, jogging, running, swimming, or whatever your primary care doctor says is safe for you to do. Increase your daily exercise gradually until you are exercising thirty minutes every day.

If you cannot seem to get yourself to start exercising, start at five minutes per day and work your way up. Anybody can exercise for five minutes! After you get started, it will be easier to continue, and soon you will be exercising enough to feel better. Do not demur because you feel you do not have enough energy to exercise, because regular exercise will help increase your energy. If you do not have the motivation to exercise, ask your doctor and therapist to help you. You'll be glad you did.

Once you are in shape, you can extend your exercise time if you wish. Do not throw yourself into your exercise program so hard that you are injured or burn out quickly. Remember, this is not an exercise contest. Your goal is to establish a regular, relaxing, sustainable daily exercise schedule that is right for you.

Is depression affecting my sleep?

Unipolar major depression causes sleep disturbances. Typically, you may have difficulty going to sleep, or you may wake too early in the morning and have difficulty getting back to sleep. Depression disrupts the normal cycle of light sleep, dreaming sleep (called rapid eye movement or REM sleep), and dreamless, restful sleep (called deep or slow-wave sleep). These types of sleep must start and stop at specific times during the night for you to have restful sleep.

Sleep-deprived and depressed individuals show similar abnormal sleep cycles; they begin their dreaming sleep cycle too early in the night. Alcohol, sedatives, and most sleeping pills disturb your sleep cycle even more. Antidepressants can help you normalize your sleep cycle, and you should return to a normal sleep cycle as your depression lifts.

Lack of sleep can directly affect your health—the inability to sleep causes a physical stress reaction, increasing adrenaline, heart rate, and blood pressure. Individuals who do not sleep well are more likely to have accidents, seizures, and violent behavior. Individuals with chronic sleep problems are more likely to get infections than those who sleep well.

Someday you may meet a doctor or advisor who will encourage you to stay up twenty-four hours without sleeping as a "cure" for unipolar major depression. Please do not do this. Some people feel better the next day, but abnormal sleep habits are bad for your mind and body.

Are my repetitive thoughts keeping me awake?

Depression causes negative thoughts to come into your mind when you do not want them. During the day, it is easier to drown out these thoughts by staying active and keeping your mind busy. When you try to fall asleep, there are no distractions or activities to drown out these intrusive thoughts, and you are at their mercy.

This can be one of the most frustrating effects of depression. Try some of the simple interventions covered in the next few pages to help you get to sleep and stay asleep.

What is "sleep hygiene?"

If you are getting sufficient exercise and appropriate nutrition and you still cannot sleep, check your sleeping habits, also called sleep hygiene.

Start by looking at your sleeping environment. Is your bedroom dark enough? If not, close the shades, or wear a sleep mask. Is your bedroom kept at a temperature conducive to sleeping? If not, turn on the heater, get a fan, or fix the air conditioner. Is your bed too hard, too soft, too short, or too shaky? Get a new mattress, or move to the couch.

You cannot expect to sleep well if you are disturbed during the night, especially when you have unipolar major depression. If the ambient noise level is too high for you, turn on a fan or buy a cheap background sound generator from the local electronics store.

If you have a baby, see if your spouse will take the night shift while you are depressed. If you have older children who wake you up or invade your bed, this is a good time to wean them of these habits. Are you disturbed at night by a snoring, kicking, or sprawling spouse? Move *them* to the couch.

If you have neighbors or housemates that stay up all night playing music, listening to loud television, or clanking around, either get them to stop, buy some earplugs, or start bunking at your friend's place. You need your sleep in order to get well.

What do I do if it feels like my body simply doesn't want to sleep?

Set aside thirty to sixty minutes before bedtime to unwind from your day, and go to bed at a reasonable hour. To ensure that there is nothing physiological blocking your sleep, do not drink caffeine or alcohol in the afternoon or evening. Some people find that a hot shower or mild exercise helps them fall asleep. Don't eat right before bedtime. In addition to throwing off your sleep cycle, you are likely to gain weight.

What medications can safely help me sleep?

If you have taken all the healthy steps above and you still are unable to sleep soundly, you may want to take something to help you sleep. Do not drink alcohol to get to sleep. Alcohol just makes you wake up early in the morning and makes it harder to get to sleep tomorrow. In fact, alcohol is one of the biggest causes of sleep problems in this country.

Furthermore, over-the-counter sleeping pills and "PM" products from the drugstore probably do more harm than good. It would be an easy thing to get a prescription sedative or hypnotic (sleeping pill) from your doctor, but you should think before taking these medications. They can further disturb your sleep cycle, cause daytime sedation, and impair your memory, among other things (see Chapter 7, What If Your Antidepressant Doesn't Work?, for more information on sedatives).

The best solution for improving sleep that is disturbed by unipolar major depression is to strengthen your medical and psychotherapeutic treatment and get well faster. If you really need something to help make you sleepy while you heal, try Benadryl (diphenhydramine), an antihistamine available over the counter at your drugstore, or Desyrel (trazodone), a prescription antidepressant that also helps bring on sleep. Neither medication is licensed as a sleeping pill.

How does my diet affect my depression?

A poor diet doesn't cause unipolar major depression, but inadequate nutrition can result in deficiencies of amino acids, fatty acids, vitamins, and minerals that impair your health, upset bodily processes, disturb the function and growth of brain cells, and worsen your depressive symptoms. Being overweight or underweight can cause psychological discomfort in the short term and can truncate your life in the long term.

What are some good, basic dietary rules?

Start with the basics, and always check your diet with your doctor. In general, you should be eating three times a day, taking in about 12–25 grams of protein in the morning and an additional 12–25 grams throughout the rest of the day. You should be eating both raw and cooked green vegetables and fruit. Your diet should be low in fat. If you are on track so far, your calorie intake should match your size and physical activity; eat more if you are too thin, and less if you are overweight. Your doctor should have charts that will help you find your most natural body weight.

Can vitamins help my depression?

Taking a simple daily multivitamin supplement can help make up for any gaps in your nutrition. Most vitamins can be obtained in meals, but because of unipolar major depression, nutritious food may not seem attractive. Here are some of the important vitamins and the effects they may have on your brain and body.

- Vitamin A: Vitamin A is available from yellow and orange vegetables and dairy products, and it is essential for the health of your eyes. Do not take vitamin A in doses higher than 3,000 micrograms (10,000 units). Higher doses taken over time can cause fatigue and loss of appetite. There are several reports of sickness or mortality from taking large doses, so do not go overboard.
- Vitamin B1: Vitamin B1, also called thiamine, is found in wheat germ, beans, nuts, and meat. It helps to metabolize carbohydrates and fats. Vitamin B1 deficiency can damage cells in your brain and spinal cord, resulting in the inability to form new memories, mental confusion, delirium, muscle weakness, and loss of coordination. Consumption of alcohol and too many carbohydrates can further decrease the amount of vitamin B1 in your body.
- Vitamin B2: This vitamin, also called riboflavin, is found in eggs, cheese, wheat germ, broccoli, and spinach. Vitamin B2 helps you metabolize carbohydrates and maintain cells in your nervous system, and it also promotes healthy eyes, skin, and mouth. Taken regularly, vitamin B2 can help decrease the frequency of migraine headaches (which are common in depression), but it will not help a migraine already in progress.
- Vitamin B3: Vitamin B3 is found in meat, and your body can also manufacture it from the tryptophan found in milk and eggs. It helps to metabolize fatty acids and other compounds. A deficiency can produce diarrhea, skin rash, and in severe cases, dementia.
- Vitamin B6: Vitamin B6 is found in chicken, fish, pork, eggs, and peanuts. It helps metabolize proteins in your diet, so if you eat a lot of protein, you need plenty of vitamin B6. Insufficient vitamin B6 can cause symptoms of fatigue and low energy and a decrease in red blood cells (anemia).

- Folate: Folate is found in raw green vegetables. It helps to synthesize your DNA. Folate is necessary for normal function of your brain and nervous system. Deficiency causes symptoms like fatigue, decreased activity, and neurological problems, as well as decreased red blood cells (anemia). A folate deficiency can keep antidepressants from working well. There is a simple blood test that can measure your folate level, so discuss it with your doctor if you are concerned that you might be deficient.
- Vitamin B12: This vitamin is found in meat and fish. It is essential for brain and body health, and deficiencies can cause severe fatigue, memory problems, and psychosis in extreme cases. Insufficient B12 can also keep your antidepressant from working successfully. Note that alcohol intake and use of some medications can decrease B12 absorption from your food. There is a simple blood test for B12 levels, so if you suspect you have a problem, discuss it with your doctor.
- Vitamin C: Vitamin C is readily available from raw citrus fruits, strawberries, tomatoes, broccoli, and other foods, and vitamin C supplements can be purchased in any drugstore. Vitamin C is necessary for the body to produce the serotonin and norepinephrine that help prevent depression. Taking too much can cause kidney stones, which are no fun. You may need to take extra vitamin C if you use aspirin, oral contraceptives, or estrogen hormone supplements that reduce blood levels of vitamin C.
- Vitamin D: Vitamin D helps your brain regulate calcium, which is necessary for healthy brain cell membranes. Five to ten minutes of sunshine on your skin three times per week is enough to produce all the vitamin D you need. If you are dark-skinned or you do not go out in the sunshine, you may need extra vitamin D. Supplements containing cholecalciferol (D3) are more active than others and are preferred.

- Vitamin E: Vitamin E occurs naturally in many vegetable oils, animal products, eggs, fruits, and vegetables. There is limited evidence that vitamin E can prevent deterioration of brain and nerve cells in Parkinson's and Alzheimer's disease. Vitamin E might have the ability to help your brain increase dopamine levels.

Vitamin deficiencies can cause depressive symptoms or make it harder for your antidepressant to work. However, there are no vitamins that will cure unipolar major depression, even at huge doses, despite what you have seen on the Internet, on television, and in magazines.

Should I take something to give me more energy?

Insufficient exercise, insomnia, and poor nutrition all add to the fatigue caused by unipolar major depression. And in turn, unipolar major depression makes it more difficult to exercise, harder to sleep, and more difficult to eat appropriately. It's a vicious cycle.

Avoid the impulse to rush out and buy the flashy energy supplements hawked on television, in magazines, and over the Internet. These often contain stimulants that are harmful to your heart, and in any case, are not natural additions to your body. Instead, work to maintain the exercise, sleep, and nutrition that contribute to your overall health and help you in your medication and psychotherapy treatment. Then you will gradually regain the natural energy that has been sapped by unipolar major depression.

It is not healthy to overdrive your natural energy level in an attempt to make yourself unnaturally energetic. Just live a healthy life, and let your body produce its own energy. Please try not to put stimulants of any kind into your body.

Are herbal supplements effective?

Although all supplements' packaging states that they are not meant to treat any illness, you will see plenty of advertisements claiming that their supplement will cure your depression in just a few days. Most of these claims are lies, so do not be misled.

Here is a list of some of the many herbal products and supplements that are promoted for the treatment of your depression; they are rated for effectiveness and safety according to the best research studies available, but remember that this information is changing all the time, so please check with your doctor first.

Rating system:

Effectiveness

EEE = This product may produce a noticeable improvement in your depression.

EE = This product may produce a mild or barely noticeable improvement in your depression.

E = This product is unlikely to produce any improvement in your depression.

Safety

SSS = This product is probably safe and beneficial for your overall health.

SS = This product is probably safe.

S = This product has significant side effects, or adequate safety information is missing.

X = This product has serious side effects, and you should avoid it altogether.

- Omega-3 Fatty Acids (EEE/SSS): Omega-3 fatty acids may be your best bet among supplements to help your fight against depression. Brain cells and their membranes contain omega-3s, and a component of omega-3s called arachidonic acid may have some activity as a brain neurochemical. However, your body cannot make omega-3s and you must obtain your supply from your diet.

  Some studies indicate that the consumption of omega-3 fatty acids might help depression, and there is even research showing that omega-3s can increase the effectiveness of antidepressants if they are taken together. These polyunsaturated fatty acids are recommended by the American Heart Association to prevent heart attacks and lower effects of cholesterol, which is also good. Omega-3s appear to reduce inflammation and stabilize cell membranes, similar to some of the new antidepressants that are currently being tested (see Chapter 7, What If Your Antidepressant Doesn't Work?, for more information on new antidepressants).

  The most important compounds in omega-3s are EPA (eicosapentanoic acid) and DHA (docosahexanoic acid), which can be found in salmon, trout, herring, and kippers. Shrimp and scallops also contain omega-3s, but at lower doses. The best way to get these oils is to include lots of fish in your diet. Oil from the evening primrose contains omega-3s in the form of linolenic acids. Walnuts, currant seed, and grape seed contain fatty acids that might also be helpful. Unfortunately, most cooking oils contain only omega-6 fatty acids, which are no help for your depression.
- Lecithin (EE/SSS): Lecithin is sometimes promoted for depression on the Internet, and it has been tried for the treatment of Alzheimer's disease, liver disease, and gall bladder disorder. The body turns it into an important neurochemical called

acetylcholine, as well as inositol and linolenic acid (see omega-3 fatty acids, choline, and inositol in this section). Lecithin is used in food preparation and is generally recognized as safe in moderate doses. It has shown some influence on depressed patients' moods and thinking efficiency.

- Lemon Balm (EE/SSS): Lemon balm (*Melissa officinalis*) has sedative effects and may help relaxation and sleep. Some studies suggest it acts like acetylcholine and may cause sedation. Lemon balm has a soothing and pleasant fragrance. It is used in foods, is generally recognized as safe in moderate amounts, and can be very effective for mild relaxation.

- Inositol (EE/SS): Inositol (also called cyclohexanehexol) is manufactured by your body and can also be obtained from melons, oranges, bran, and supplements. Inositol is an important component of brain cells, and the brains of depressed individuals and suicide victims show a deficit in inositol. It seems promising as a depression treatment, but we do not yet know enough about it to be sure.

- SAMe (EEE/S): SAMe (s-adenosyl-methionine) can improve your mood, and it can reduce symptoms of depression. There is evidence that SAMe may increase serotonin, norepinephrine, and dopamine like traditional antidepressants. It also may have anti-inflammatory effects. Current studies suggest that it is safe, but the research on SAMe is plagued by flawed study designs and poorly diagnosed research subjects. At this time we do not know whether SAMe is safe or not, especially if you take it for a long time.

  SAMe can cause side effects of nausea, dizziness, headache, insomnia, nervousness, sweating, and vomiting. It should not be given to individuals with bipolar depression, because mania and suicidality may result. SAMe may help provoke the rare "serotonin syndrome" if combined with other serotonin drugs (see Chapter 5, Newer Antidepressant Medications, for more on serotonin syndrome).

- St. John's Wort (EE/S): Some studies of St. John's wort (*Hypericum perforatum*) show that it can relieve symptoms of mild depression. Unfortunately, most of these studies were small, and the patients did not receive a careful diagnosis. In a large study using carefully diagnosed patients, St. John's wort produced no significant improvement in unipolar major depression.

  It is not yet clear exactly what St. John's wort does in your body. Some studies suggest that it increases serotonin and may have some effects on norepinephrine and dopamine. Other researchers claim that it exerts its main effects on a neurochemical called gamma aminobutyric acid (GABA) or has an MAOI effect.

  Probably the worst problem with St. John's wort is that it makes your skin more sensitive to the effects of sunlight, which can increase your risk for skin cancer, especially if you live in states that get a lot of sunshine in the summer. St. John's wort can decrease the hormones in oral contraceptives, and abnormal menstruation and unplanned pregnancies have been reported after its use. It can also cause sexual dysfunction.

  St. John's wort should not be taken with antidepressants or other medications that increase serotonin. This includes Imitrex (sumatriptan) and other migraine medications. It should be avoided if you are taking Demerol (meperidine), Ultram (tramadol), or other opiates. Check with your doctor to see if you are taking any contraindicated medications before starting St. John's wort.

- Passionflower (E/S): Extract of the passionflower (*Passiflora incarnata*) has a mild sedative effect that may be useful for insomnia or agitation. Its mechanism and safety are not known, and it can cause dizziness and confusion in some individuals.

- Panax Ginseng (E/S): As far as depression treatment goes, *Panax ginseng* (also called Korean or red ginseng) just seems to be a stimulant. Like other familiar stimulants such as caffeine, *Panax* can improve mood as well as cause anxiety, agitation, insomnia, and an abnormal heartbeat. Beware of taking *Panax* with other stimulants like coffee, tea, guarana, country mallow, or bitter orange, which together may cause increased blood pressure or heart arrhythmia. For similar reasons, be careful taking *Panax* with antidepressants, especially MAOIs. In individuals with bipolar depression, *Panax* can trigger euphoria, mania, and psychosis. It can also change hormone levels, and some women have had swollen, painful breasts after taking it.

  The purpose of depression treatment is to return your mind and body to its most natural state, not to jack it up with unnatural stimulation. Stimulants do not help unipolar major depression, and you should stay away from them.

- Choline (E/SSS): Choline (trimethylethanolamine) is contained in meat, fish, liver, eggs, nuts, and other foods. Human breast milk contains choline; it is added to artificial baby formulas, and it may help in early brain development. It can produce unpleasant symptoms of sweating, stomachache, vomiting, and diarrhea; it's also not known for helping depression. You may want to look elsewhere for a supplement.

- Tyrosine (E/SS): Although tyrosine in the body is converted into norepinephrine and dopamine, adding *extra* tyrosine in a supplement does not increase brain levels of either of these neurochemicals. For this reason, tyrosine is unlikely to help your depression.

- Phenylalanine (E/SS): Phenylalanine is an amino acid that is being promoted for the treatment of depression, mostly based on limited studies performed twenty years ago. It is converted by the body into tyrosine, which, unfortunately, provides little benefit for depression (see tyrosine, above).

- 5-HTP (EE/X): 5-HTP (5-hydroxytryptophan) is converted into serotonin, which is needed in unipolar major depression. Some studies show that 5-HTP reduces depressive symptoms, but it can also cause heartburn, stomach reflux, nausea, stomachache, vomiting, and diarrhea.

  Doctors are concerned that commercially available 5-HTP can cause a potentially fatal condition called eosinophilia myalgia syndrome with symptoms of extreme muscle pain, joint pain, hair loss, rash, and fatigue that may not go away. If you want to increase serotonin in your brain, you are better off taking antidepressants with a clear safety record and avoiding 5-HTP until these concerns are resolved.

- Tryptophan (EE/X): The body converts tryptophan to 5-HTP and then into serotonin within the brain, improving depressive symptoms. Unfortunately, there have been more than 1,500 potentially fatal cases of eosinophilia myalgia syndrome. Thirty-seven deaths have been caused by synthetic tryptophan in the United States so far. For this reason, avoid tryptophan supplements.

- DHEA (E/X): DHEA (dihydroepiandrosterone) is heavily promoted by magazines and books as a treatment for depression. Many people who take it report an improved sense of well-being and more energy, even if they do not suffer from unipolar major depression. However, some of the positive feelings associated with DHEA are likely just the short-term effects of the steroid hormones that are produced when DHEA is broken down within the body.

Steroid hormones can contribute to brain cell death and aggravate depression in the long term. DHEA should not be taken lightly, as it can affect your hormonal balance, increasing male sex hormones in women and boosting female sex hormones in men. Adequate safety testing is absent, and most safety information only covers DHEA use for a few weeks. There is also some concern that taking DHEA may contribute to breast cancer and prostate cancer. Be very careful and consult with your doctor if you decide to take DHEA.

- Kava (E/X): Kava is the extract of a pepper (*Piper methysticum*). It is sedating at moderate doses and intoxicating at higher doses. It has been widely recommended in the popular press as a treatment for anxiety, although its mechanism of action is not clear. It can cause side effects of allergic skin rashes and eye irritation. However, the most important information about kava is that liver toxicity and liver failure have been reported in individuals taking normal doses for just a short time. Stay away from kava.
- Hawaiian Baby Wood Rose (E/X): Often listed as a potential treatment for depression, Hawaiian baby wood rose (*Asplenium scolopendrium*) contains hallucinogens such as ergonovine and other related chemicals that should not be taken in an uncontrolled fashion. In addition, ingestion of this product can cause nausea, vomiting, dizziness, increased heart rate, and increased blood pressure. Avoid it.

Is it safe to buy supplements from the Internet?

Unfortunately, there are no nationally enforced standards for supplements, and it is hard to know exactly what you are getting over the Internet. The FDA has many examples of Internet supplements that contained the wrong ingredients (including undisclosed drugs like Viagra), outdated ingredients, dirt, or filth ranging from insect parts to rodent hairs. If you buy supplements, get them in person from a dealer that you trust.

Are drug companies suppressing natural products to make more money from their drugs?

It's often said that pharmaceutical corporations are trying to keep supplements off the market so that they can make money by selling their prescription drugs. Nothing is farther from the truth. Drug companies are always looking for ways to make money. If any drug company thought they had found a naturally occurring supplement that treated depression successfully and would pass the U.S. Food and Drug Administration's stringent safety tests, you can bet they would have found some way to package it and sell it as a prescription drug. For example, when studies found that human growth hormone improved sleep, a pharmaceutical company quickly patented it in a new form and sold it as a prescription sleeping pill called Rozerem (ramelteon). When studies showed that the amino acid called homotaurine helped reduce alcohol intake, a pharmaceutical company quickly patented a similar chemical, which is now being sold as a prescription drug called Campral (acamprosate).

What are some commonly used products that are bad for my depression?

You should generally avoid stimulants and any product that is addicting. Here are some of the products you should think about cutting back on, or quitting altogether.

- Caffeine: Caffeine is powerfully addicting, and it can cause insomnia, stomach irritation, increased heart rate, increased urination, increased perspiration, and unnecessary nervousness. Even so-called healthy products like power drinks, energy drinks, sports drinks, and "vitamin fortified water" frequently contain caffeine or conceal it in substances like guarana extract (*Paullinia cupana*). You may not even realize that you are addicted to such a common substance, but if you are consuming lots of beverages that contain caffeine, it's likely that you are. Switch to noncaffeinated versions, or taper yourself off altogether.

- Chocolate: Chocolate contains caffeine as well as other stimulants like phenylethylamine, theobromine, and theophylline, which cause problems in large doses. If you binge on chocolate when you are depressed (you know who you are!) try to wean yourself of this habit. If you need help, ask your doctor or therapist.

- Tobacco: Using tobacco on top of an antidepressant can decrease the amount of the drug that gets to your blood and brain, sabotaging your attempts to fight depression. Using tobacco in any form causes cancer, and breathing it into the lungs contributes to lung problems and heart failure. Half of the people smoking now will die of tobacco-related causes. Talk to your doctor and therapist about how to quit.

    If you want to try to quit on your own, try controlled regression. Start by counting the number of cigarettes you smoke a day, and put that number into a pack or cigarette case every morning. Every day, smoke every cigarette in the pack, but no more. Every week, put one less cigarette in the pack. Soon you will be reducing your risk of health problems, and you will be on the way to a permanent cessation that you can maintain.

- Alcohol: It's honestly best if no one who is currently depressed or has ever been depressed drinks more than one cocktail, glass of wine, or bottle of beer per week. There are some individuals who are so sensitive that one drink a week may be too much.

Alcohol in any form is poisonous to brain cells, and brain cell damage is one of the things we are fighting to stop your depression. It does not make any sense for you to work hard on your depression treatment and then kill a bunch of your brain cells for the sake of a pleasant afternoon or evening. If you have trouble stopping or you are concerned that you may have a drinking problem, talk to your doctor and therapist, and remember that one of the most effective sources of help is Alcoholics Anonymous.

• Illegal Drugs: Recreational drugs are generally bad for your depression. Methamphetamine, cocaine, and other, similar illegal drugs make depression worse, as well as putting you at risk for being arrested.

What about marijuana? It makes me feel less depressed after I smoke it.

The general feeling among physicians is that marijuana makes depression worse in the long run. Marijuana smoking produces stimulation that morphs into sedation. It may interfere with the effectiveness of antidepressants by changing chemicals in your brain. Smoking dope may make you feel better now, but it will make it harder for you to get out of your depression in the end.

Chapter 13

STRESS-REDUCTION TECHNIQUES

What exactly is stress?

Stress refers to any event that triggers your brain's stress reaction, releasing stress steroid hormones and activating neurochemicals in your brain. These stress steroids and activating neurochemicals damage and kill brain cells and can throw you into an episode of depression. There is good evidence that the stress response also contributes to heart disease, lung disease, and other problems that can cause us to die too soon.

Stress is additive, meaning that several small stressors can add up to a big one. Here are examples of the most common stressful events.

- Death of a child or marriage partner
- Breakup of a marriage or a close relationship
- Sickness or death of any loved one
- Alcohol problems or drug addiction
- Serious illness or injury
- Severe financial problems
- Arguments and strife at home or work
- Demotion or loss of job
- Son or daughter leaving home
- Spiritual and religious conflict
- Disappointments and failure to achieve life goals
- Overwork
- Moving

Why do I get depressed over happy events, like my wedding?

Weddings are happy occasions, but the physical and emotional demands of a wedding can provoke your body's stress reaction, releasing damaging stress hormones into your brain and triggering your depression. Some other pleasant occasions like birthdays, anniversaries, and vacations can initiate the stress response as well. It really does not matter whether an event is pleasant or unpleasant; if it triggers your body's stress response, the resulting brain injury can activate your unipolar major depression.

Is there somewhere I can go to get away from stress?

If you lived in a hollow tree deep in the redwood forest, you might not have become depressed in the first place. Depressive patients have moved to sparsely populated areas, built their own homes, home-schooled their children, and become more self-sufficient, and they have felt better after reducing their stress. However, most of us choose to live in a more challenging, more stressful world, and we must rely on stress-reduction strategies to keep healthy.

Is there something simple and easy I can try to reduce my stress level?

Sure; try giving yourself a break. Everybody's daily routine tends to get dull and annoying with time, and depression just makes it worse. It is just common sense to take a break from your daily activities.

A break does not have to be a skiing trip to the Himalayas. Just take ten minutes from your day and escape from your usual routine. At work or school, you can schedule a walk around the block or go to a quiet spot and listen to music. See if you can expand this single break into two or three intervals per day. Try breaking up your daily routine by going out to lunch. Try taking the stairs at your home, school, or workplace instead of using the elevator.

When you are not working, reserve time for nonproductive activities that you enjoy (or used to enjoy). Why not take a long, hot bath or shower tonight? Let yourself soak up the water until you relax. Try taking a brief nap. Eat something special for dinner. Spend some time reading, listening to music, playing a musical instrument, watching a movie, playing with a pet, taking a walk, running, or riding your bicycle. If you play tennis, golf, or some other active sport, make sure that you set aside some time every week for these activities. It is not a question of whether you have time to do these things; the reality is that you have to engage in these activities if you want your depression to end (see the Pleasant Events Program on page 246).

What else can I do?

If you can't work breaks into your busy schedule, why not reward yourself a little bit? It is very easy. Just pick an amount of money that is appropriate to your means, from $5 to $100; it really does not matter. Now make a commitment to spend this money each week on purchasing something fun and enjoyable for yourself. It could be a candy bar, a DVD, a book, a pair of shoes, or whatever you otherwise would not have given yourself. When you enjoy your reward, remember that you are not such a bad person after all, and with some work and a lot of common sense, you'll soon feel right as rain.

If I reduce the stress in my life, will I really feel better?

If you could completely relax your body and quiet your thoughts, you would immediately feel better. If you do not know how to relax your body and mind, you should learn some exercises that will help you calm your own stress response. This will speed up your recovery from depression and reduce the likelihood that you will become depressed again.

People have been using relaxation and meditation exercises to reduce stress for several thousand years. Practice your relaxation exercise every day, and use it when you know you will be subjected to extra stress, such as having to make a presentation or meet a deadline. When you fall into depression's black pit, try using your relaxation exercise to help you climb out of the morass. Best of all, relaxation exercises are easy to learn and pleasant to do.

What are muscle relaxation techniques?

Muscle relaxation exercises relax your body and mind, giving you an opportunity to recover from the excess norepinephrine and steroid stress hormones that are part of your stressful life. When you are totally relaxed, you will experience some immediate relief from your depression. You can learn relaxation techniques from behavioral psychotherapists or you can try this one on your own.

Start by sitting comfortably in a chair or lying down. Breathe in and out slowly a few times. Now slowly take a deep breath as you contract all the muscles in your toes, feet, and legs. Hold your breath a moment while you keep your muscles tight, then breathe out slowly and relax your muscles. Take another deep, slow breath while you tighten all the muscles in your abdomen, shoulders, arms, and fingers. Hold your breath for a moment while keeping your muscles tight, then breathe out, and relax them. Now take another long, slow breath in while tightening the muscles in your neck and face. Hold this breath for a moment while keeping your muscles tight, then breathe out, and relax all your muscles. Now notice your breathing. As you slowly breathe in, imagine you are gathering all the stress in your body. Then breathe out slowly, and exhale all your stress along with your breath. Continue this breathing for a minute or longer if you like, until you can feel that your body and mind have relaxed. Use this muscle relaxation technique twice a day, or any time that you will have to deal with a stressful event.

Can meditation help my depression?

Meditation is a collection of physical, mental, emotional, and spiritual exercises that have been developed over the last few thousand years. In addition to relieving stress, meditation can strengthen your control over thoughts and emotions and increase your ability to manage your own depression. You can also use meditation to increase your alertness, improve your concentration, and become aware of your real self that's buried under depression.

Can I meditate just by breathing a certain way?

In a wonderful, simple meditation, you simply sit and listen to your breath. Start by sitting down and getting comfortable. Now breathe in, and slowly count to seven while you try to feel and listen to the breath entering your body. Now exhale slowly as you hear and feel your breath flowing out of your lungs, leaving your nose, and going out into the world again. Repeat this, and let the sound and feeling capture your attention so that thoughts and the outside world disappear. Continue listening, feeling, and breathing slowly in and out, like the tide. Do this for just thirty seconds twice a day. If you wish, you may slowly increase the duration every week. Many people like to do this meditation in the morning immediately after waking and at night, just before falling asleep. You can also perform this simple exercise at work, at school, or anywhere you are going to face stress.

Please do not push yourself in this technique. There are no prizes for a good performance. The rewards are relaxation, health, and inner peace.

Is there a stronger form of meditation that is easy to do?

Another meditation simply involves focusing your attention on two crossed lines. Carefully remove page 172 containing the "meditation card," paste it on light cardboard, and cut it out. You may want to make up a bunch of these cards so you can keep one in every place you might need it.

When you want to use the card, either hold it in your hand or lay it on a flat surface. Notice the two crossed lines, and find the tiny spot where they cross. This is where your attention is going to go. Fix your eyes and concentration on this spot, and do not let your focus wander from it. If you hear something that distracts your attention, shift your focus back to the spot as soon as you notice it has strayed. As soon as a thought comes into your mind, just redirect your focus back to the little spot.

Try thinking of the spot as a tiny black hole that pulls everything into it. If you notice a distracting thought, mentally drag it to the hole, where it is sucked in and carried away. Try this for thirty seconds twice a day at first. After that, you can increase the time gradually if you wish.

Carry the meditation card with you, and use it before stressful meetings, speeches, classes, tests, or anywhere else you need focus and relief from stress. The card is so small that you can use it anywhere without being noticed. Put a copy in your wallet or purse, and keep another copy on your desk or work area. Use the meditation card to help you focus before starting your work, to help you relax after coming home, and to calm down before bedtime so you can get a restful night's sleep.

The Meditation Card

This card will help you control your mind. Look at the crossed lines and find the spot where they intersect. Focus all your attention on this spot. If you are distracted, just redirect your focus to the spot again. Do this for thirty seconds, twice a day, or whenever you need to relax and reduce stress.

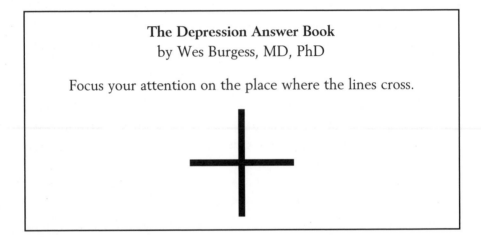

The Depression Answer Book
by Wes Burgess, MD, PhD

Focus your attention on the place where the lines cross.

What's the best type of meditation for curbing intrusive, negative thoughts?

The best type of meditation for getting control of intrusive thoughts is simply called sitting. In principle, sitting meditation is the simplest thing in the world. You just sit down and let all the thoughts drop from your mind. People who practice sitting can maintain a clear mind with no thoughts for minutes at a time or longer. Some experienced meditators can keep their minds clear of thoughts for hours wherever they are.

Sitting is an excellent technique to learn, because it is an instant antidepressant. If you are like most depressed meditators, as soon as the thoughts drop from your mind, your depression will fall away with them. It is a wonderful experience to obtain relief from your depression suddenly and completely, if only for a moment.

How can I try sitting meditation?

Start by settling on a chair or the floor in a comfortable position, facing a blank wall. Zen masters sit with legs folded and posture erect, but for you, just sitting comfortably is fine. Sit about one to three feet from the wall. Let your eyelids partially close, and simply begin to notice yourself. Without moving, be aware of your toes, feet, legs, elbows, eyes, nose, and mouth. Listen to the breath coming into and leaving your body. Notice what is coming into your mind, and whenever a thought comes into your mind, notice it and look for the next thought. Soon, the next thought will not come, and you will notice that your mind is clear of distractions. Do this twice a day for thirty to sixty seconds. If you want, you can gradually increase the amount of time after that.

A few people can go for longer periods of time right away, but most need a bit of practice. At first, you will find yourself constantly distracted until you finally have a clear moment when all your thoughts drop away. This will probably be a new experience for you, and it can be dramatic. Little by little, as you practice, your clear moments will become longer and more frequent, until you can maintain a clear mind for minutes at a time.

If you want to pursue this sitting technique, there are many excellent teachers available to help you. Although sitting meditation is often associated with Zen Buddhism, it is not restricted to any religion. You should be able to find teachers and resources that are easily compatible with your personal beliefs.

Is there some way other than meditation to help me stop these intrusive thoughts?

If you want another way to shut down unwanted thoughts, you can take advantage of the fact that your subconscious mind is interested in your welfare and will be cooperative with your efforts to feel better. Your unpleasant thoughts are not under your conscious control—if they were, you would just will them away and they would disappear. Instead, they are under the control of your subconscious mind, which, unfortunately, is pretty out of touch and does not know what you want it to do.

To enlist help from your subconscious mind, you must first get its attention. There are two good ways to do this: the first is to wear a rubber band around your wrist. It should be quite loose on your arm; we do not want you to turn blue. When you want to get your subconscious mind's attention, just stretch the rubber band an inch or two and let it snap back on your wrist. Use only enough pressure to attract your attention, but do not snap it hard on your wrist. Remember, this is a psychological exercise, not self-torture by rubber band. Practice until you can apply the right amount of stretch to produce just the right snap.

Some people find this to be too conspicuous, or they just do not like snapping themselves with rubber bands. If this is you, try the second attention-getting device. Take the first inch of the tip of your left thumb between the thumb and first finger of your right hand, and give it a squeeze. You will quickly find that you can deliver just enough pressure to capture your attention. You can do this in your lap while in a meeting or even behind your back, if you do not want anyone to notice.

Now, apply your signal, and simply tell your subconscious what you want it to do. Softly say aloud, "I do not need to think about my brother's illness now." Or say, "I prefer not to think about my finances," or even "I don't want any more thoughts about my weight." Whatever intrusive thought is bothering you the most, tell yourself what you want to do with it. It helps if you use the same words each time.

Now you are all set. Whenever you notice the intrusive thought come into your mind, give the signal and speak your message aloud or under your breath. Gradually, you will notice that the intrusive thought you are working on stops coming into your mind. You can also use this same technique to block anxious habits like sniffing, coughing, or biting your nails. Just pick a message to tell your subconscious mind, and whenever you notice the habit, apply your signal and say the message to yourself. It is amazing how well this technique works despite the fact that it seems rather silly at first.

What if I can't relax, even with these techniques?

If you do these exercises and they do not give you relief, you need to take a hard look at how much stress you are experiencing on a daily basis. If you are working too much or too long, you may need to cut down. If you are constantly in conflict with someone in your life, you may have to take a break from them for a while, even if they are important to you. If you are overwhelmed with self-criticism and worn out by a constant string of losses, disappointments, and failures, you may need a rest away from life stresses until you have begun to put this depression behind you. A depressed person has to know his limits; don't try to go beyond them until you feel better. If you need help or suggestions on what to reduce, talk with your family, friends, doctor, and therapist.

If you cannot do any of these exercises at all, then your depression needs to be better controlled in order for you to recover. Ask your doctor what antidepressants can stop your intrusive thoughts.

Chapter 14

WOMEN AND DEPRESSION

- Why is depression different for a woman?
- How can I handle all my responsibilities when I'm depressed?
- What do other women do when their menstrual cycle makes their depression worse?
- Will my depression worsen during menopause?
- Will I pass my depression on to my unborn child?
- Can I keep taking my antidepressants during pregnancy?
- What do other women do about their depression while they are pregnant?
- What can I do to make sure my pregnancy goes perfectly?
- What can I do to avoid postpartum depression?
- Might severe postpartum depression turn into mania?
- How can I keep the fear of losing my baby from overwhelming me?
- Can I breast-feed while I'm on antidepressants?
- How do I regain my appetite? I'm starting to look sickly from weight loss.
- What are some easy ways to make sure I'm getting the nutrition I need?
- How do I avoid putting on weight when I'm depressed?
- Will diet pills interfere with my health or make my depression worse?
- How else can I combat simultaneous depression and weight problems?
- What can I do about my loss of interest in sex?
- Is it normal that my sexuality seems to have changed?
- Depression has made me feel distant from my partner—should I act on these feelings?
- What do I do if my depressed partner won't get treatment?
- Why has my partner become unreasonably demanding and physical since my depression began?
- My depression increases whenever I look in the mirror—what can I do to feel better about my appearance?
- How can I help my depressed friend feel better about herself?
- Where can I find more help on women and depression?

Why is depression different for a woman?

More than twice as many women are given the diagnosis of major depression than men, and their depression is usually more complicated. As a depressed woman, in addition to changes in mood, your depression is more likely to affect your sense of self, your feelings about your body, and your ability to support and nurture others. You are more vulnerable to being depressed during times of natural hormonal fluctuations such as your menstrual period. Your depression can affect your desire to have children, your physical and emotional health during and after pregnancy, and whether you choose to breastfeed. Unfortunately, our culture currently provides few opportunities for women to extend and receive support from other depressed women who have already passed through these challenges.

How can I handle all my responsibilities when I'm depressed?

In the past, you have probably provided help and emotional support for family, friends, and workmates. Now the situation is reversed, and you need their help. Start by informing others in your life that you need their consideration and support. You may have to tell your friends and family not to be so needy. You may have to explain to your boss that you cannot work so hard or for such long hours. Most of all, you need to be judicious with yourself and stop trying to help everyone else all the time. Now is the time when you have to help yourself.

Once you have a little breathing room, sit back and start to think of the things you still can do, instead of what you can't. Use the relaxation exercises in Chapter 13, Stress-Reduction Techniques, and the Life Activation Worksheet on page 248 to reacquaint yourself with what is good in your life.

If you still have too many responsibilities, make sure that you stake out some time during the day that you can call your own. Do not worry or feel guilty if you need to spend some time alone or with a friend to feel better. You need this time to calm your mind. Call on your mother, sister, or friend to help lighten your load (e.g., by taking care of your children for an afternoon). When you feel the need for company, try to find low-pressure activities where you can relax and be yourself. Try to avoid activities that you have to plan or supervise. Try going out to a movie, the beach, a concert, a ball game, or another simple event that will let you choose your level of participation. Use the Pleasant Events Program on page 246 to help you schedule activities where you can spend time with supportive people and renew close relationships.

What do other women do when their menstrual cycle makes their depression worse?

Depressed women's premenstrual cycles often worsen their depression, and their menses are often quite painful. Fortunately, some antidepressants treat both PMS and depression at the same time. Zoloft (sertraline) can be used to treat both—if you find that it helps, you can stay on it to both keep control over your PMS and keep unipolar major depressive episodes from returning.

Decreasing body fluid helps reduce cramping for many women. Reducing salt in your diet, exercising, gentle swimming, and soaking in a hot tub all help your body reduce excess body fluid. The tricyclic antidepressants Tofranil (imipramine) and Pamelor (nortriptyline) decrease body fluid and reduce both depression symptoms and PMS for many women.

Will my depression worsen during menopause?

The passage into the third trimester of life should bring a sense of satisfaction and fulfillment. In other cultures, female maturity brings with it the authority of wisdom and the responsibility of leadership among other women. However, our culture is obsessed with youth, and too often, menopause brings the stigma of age, infertility, and incapacity. Women may lose a sense of their own body image and be discontented with what is, ultimately, a perfectly natural process into maturity.

Menopause does not have to be viewed through the distorted lens of our youth-obsessed culture. Most of the time, menopause usually does not trigger or worsen unipolar major depression, and it may even provide some protection against depressive episodes. If you are one of the women who have a depressive episode when your cycling changes, it should be evaluated and treated the same as it would be during other periods of your life.

Estrogen replacement alone can provide relief of vasomotor symptoms, minor cognitive complaints, and mild mood symptoms, and it is also useful in preventing osteoporosis. However, estrogen usually does not relieve unipolar major depression. For that, as you know, you need antidepressant therapy, psychotherapy, and healthy life habits. If you become depressed during menopause, do not automatically assume that it's responsible; you may wish to see your doctor and/or therapist for evaluation.

Will I pass my depression on to my unborn child?

There are genetic risks of passing on depression (see Chapter 3, Diagnosis and Causes), but pregnancy is more than a question of genetics. The world desperately needs more honest, sincere, loving people. Will your child be able to feed on your love and return it to others throughout his or her life? Meditate on these issues, pray, or talk to the people whose advice you trust the most. Most of all, you must look inside your heart for the answer. Depression should not stop you from having a child if you are ready for the burdens and rewards of parenthood.

Remember, your children may or may not develop unipolar major depression. If they do, your depression gives you the ideal understanding and ability to give them the extra help, nurturance, and early treatment they need to ameliorate the effects of depression later in life.

Can I keep taking my antidepressants during pregnancy?

The first thing to do is find out if your depression can be controlled with psychotherapy alone. If you are already in psychotherapy, continue with it. If you are using psychotherapy along with medications to treat your depression, see if you can lower the medications or taper them away. If you are not yet working with a psychotherapist, this is the time to start. Try to give yourself enough time to develop a healthy therapeutic relationship before you become pregnant.

If you find that you still require some medications, take the lowest doses possible to control your unipolar major depression. Find out the risks of your current antidepressants for pregnancy, and if there are others that are safer, consider changing to one of these.

You already know that taking medications during pregnancy can increase the risk of birth problems. However, there are also risks if you stop your depression treatment. If you abruptly stop taking an antidepressant before pregnancy, you run a high risk of your depression returning while you are pregnant. Never stop antidepressants suddenly, because this may help trigger a sudden episode of unipolar major depression.

If you have been considering stopping your treatment and just suffering with your depression symptoms during the nine long months of your pregnancy, don't. While you are actively depressed, you are more likely to fall, crash your car, or have some other accident that could endanger you and the baby. You will be more likely to have an infection, particularly a viral infection during your pregnancy, if you are depressed. Some doctors even believe that the extra steroid stress hormones and excitatory neurochemicals that women experience while they are depressed can affect the gestation or the preterm development of your child.

What do other women do about their depression while they are pregnant?

The best and most successful course of action is to gather a team of professionals who agree to communicate and work together to support your pregnancy. This team could consist of a family practice doctor and your psychotherapist, or a pediatrician, an obstetrician, and a psychiatrist. Pick one member of the team to coordinate all your efforts and communicate your wishes to the other members.

If your depression is controlled with psychotherapy, make advance arrangements with your therapist to continue your sessions by telephone or the Internet if you cannot leave your home or you are in the hospital. If medications are needed, ask your team what's best for you and the baby while you search the Internet to discover all the latest information on the pregnancy risks of your antidepressant and potential substitutes. Working with the members of your team, make a chart of every month during your pregnancy that details the risks of medication during each period, and decide in advance what you will do if you become mildly depressed, severely depressed, or disabled by depression. The choices can include increasing your psycho-therapy, starting an antidepressant, raising or lowering doses of an antidepressant you are already taking, or changing your medications altogether. Then distribute copies of your chart to each of your team members as a reference for them to consult during your pregnancy. In this way, you will have made the best decisions in advance, and you are unlikely to become overwhelmed if you fall into an episode of unipolar major depression while you are pregnant.

What can I do to make sure my pregnancy goes perfectly?

There is no way you can remove all the risk from your life, even if you're the healthiest, happiest person in the world. Be assured that the likelihood of problems with modern birth and pregnancy is relatively low, no matter what you choose to do. The majority of depressed women have wonderful, healthy children who are born into loving families and have healthy, fulfilling lives.

What can I do to avoid postpartum depression?

Changes in hormones, relationships, and lifestyle can conspire to make you more vulnerable to negative emotions after you give birth. The "baby blues" refers to a short period of sadness that can occur after you take your baby home. However, many depressed women are uniquely prepared to deal with the baby blues, because they are already experts at controlling their mood changes.

Over 10 percent of new mothers develop classical postpartum depression four to six weeks after birth. And if you have stopped or decreased your depression treatment, you are vulnerable to it. If you have stopped your antidepressants during pregnancy, it is a good idea to restart them as soon as possible. Some clever women ask their spouses or doctors to stand by with their usual antidepressants in the birthing suite so they can take them immediately after parturition.

You can reduce the stresses of being a new mother by letting the people in your life know that things will be different after your baby is born. They should not expect you to go back to your previous schedule and responsibilities—your priorities are recovering from your pregnancy and attending to the needs of your baby. If you do notice that your depression is getting worse, do not waste time in informing your doctor and therapist so you stay ahead of any possible problems.

Might severe postpartum depression turn into mania?

It's possible, but this is much more likely to happen if you have bipolar depression, not unipolar depression. Classical postpartum depressive emergencies are more likely in women who have bipolar disorder. If your postpartum depression becomes mania, see your psychiatrist and ask her to reevaluate your diagnosis of unipolar major depression.

How can I keep the fear of losing my baby from overwhelming me?

The most important thing you can do is to refuse to live in fear. The odds are great that everything will go perfectly in your pregnancy and birth. If things are not completely perfect, you will deal with it, just as you have dealt with other challenges in your life. Do not let irrational fears and fantasies trigger or worsen your depression. Instead, experience and enjoy these events of your life moment by moment; the future will arrive soon enough on its own.

If you have any evidence that there might be a problem, it makes sense to protect yourself. Some couples choose to wait before telling all their family and friends about the pregnancy until they are sure that it will not be a complex one. Some couples wait to fix the baby's room, move furniture, and buy baby clothes until their healthy baby comes home. Do what you can to alleviate your fears, and know that, in all likelihood, you will soon have a happy, healthy baby.

Can I breast-feed while I'm on antidepressants?

Many antidepressants are released into breast milk. What's best for your baby depends on the baby's health, your emotions, and the intricacies of antidepressant physiology. Put your team of doctors to work on this question until they come up with a set of options you can use. And of course, if you can switch to psychotherapy alone to fight your depression, that will alleviate the risk.

How do I regain my appetite? I'm starting to look sickly from weight loss.

Decreased appetite caused by depression can also be influenced by our culture's constant pressure to be thin, resulting in fatigue, increased vulnerability to illness, and even malnutrition. In some women, depression can also cause the opposite—junk food bingeing and weight gain—which is just as bad. Poor nutrition or abnormal weight can work against your depression treatment, making it harder for you to get well again.

Let's start with your diet. Make sure you are getting enough protein (25–50 grams per day) from fish, chicken, milk, and beef. Also, eat plenty of raw green and yellow vegetables and fiber. Make sure you are eating enough of the right things both for sustenance and for essential nutrition. If you do not get enough nutrients from your diet, you may need to take supplements. If you have questions, ask your doctor to refer you to a nutritionist.

If you are not sure if your weight is a problem, ask your doctor to look at his height and weight charts and calculate your body mass index (BMI), which can predict health problems. If your weight has dropped so low that you lose your menstrual periods, inform your obstetrician/gynecologist or family doctor right away.

What are some easy ways to make sure I'm getting the nutrition I need?

Following are some quick nutritional tips for depressed women:

- Studies show that alcohol aggravates women's depression more than men's depression. Use extra care and moderation when drinking, especially if there is any risk that you could become pregnant.
- Recent studies show that many women have insufficient folate, especially during pregnancy. Folate may play a role in depression, so eat plenty of raw green vegetables (preferably), or take a folate supplement.
- Vitamins B6 and B12 have also been implicated in depression, so make sure you get plenty in a balanced diet. Milk is often fortified with extra vitamin B12.
- There is some recent evidence that vitamin D supplementation may reduce risk of aggressive breast cancer. Make sure you do not have a deficiency (see Chapter 12, Good Health Habits) by getting out in the sunshine for ten minutes three times a week or by taking a supplement.
- Women who suffer from unipolar major depression are more likely to develop osteoporosis and easily broken bones than nondepressed women. This may be because depression increases the levels of the body chemicals that produce inflammation. Make sure you are taking calcium supplements.
- If you are pregnant or breast-feeding and want omega-3 fatty acids in your diet, eat fish and take a supplement. Stay away from shark, swordfish, king mackerel, golden bass, and golden skipper fish, because they may contain high levels of methyl mercury.

- Do not take DHEA supplements while pregnant or breast-feeding, because they may expose your baby to high levels of male hormones.

How do I avoid putting on weight when I'm depressed?

Concentrate on cultivating a healthy lifestyle, paying special attention to your nutrition, and getting moderate exercise and satisfying sleep (see Chapter 12, Good Health Habits). If you are drawn to junk food restaurants, look for salads, take the bread off sandwiches, and try broiled, not fried, foods. If your depression is keeping you from losing weight, do not panic. You can try Weight Watchers, Jenny Craig, or other legitimate weight loss systems. Always confer with your doctor before beginning a diet or weight loss program.

Will diet pills interfere with my health or make my depression worse?

Please avoid diet pills. Prescription drugs for weight loss like Adipex and Ionamin (phentermine), Didrex (benzphetamine), and Desoxyn (methamphetamine) are addictive. They can interfere with your sleep and sabotage your depression treatment, and they may cause high blood pressure, stroke, heart arrhythmia, and heart attack.

Also, avoid over-the-counter drugstore, herbal, and vitamin products promoted for weight loss. Most of them contain stimulants that increase the secretion of stress neurochemicals. The most common ingredient is caffeine in large doses, which is not part of a healthy lifestyle. Labels and advertising can be intentionally misleading. For example, any weight loss ascribed to green tea is caused by the caffeine it contains. A product called bitter orange (*Citrus aurantium*) contains adrenaline-like chemicals called synephrine and octopamine that are similar to ephedrine.

Some heavily advertised products are more effective at removing money from your wallet than pounds from your body. For example, a product called chitosan is made from the shells of crustaceans. It is claimed to block fat absorption, but so far, studies do not show any benefit for weight loss. Another product currently promoted for weight loss, *Hoodia gordonii*, is taken from a cactus growing in the Kalahari Desert. Unfortunately, there is no reliable evidence that Hoodia is safe or effective for weight loss.

How else can I combat simultaneous depression and weight problems?

Start with Chapter 12 and develop better health habits. Exercise judiciously, and eat for nutrition. Use the stress-reduction techniques in Chapter 13 to engender inner calm and help fight the stress that makes you want to eat.

If healthy habits are not enough, two medications called Xenical and Alli (orlistat) may come in handy. Xenical is the name of the prescription form, and Alli is available over the counter. They both reduce weight by reducing the amount of dietary fat that is absorbed into your body. These drugs do not seem to interfere with depression treatment. Several women I know have been able to start exercising and going to Weight Watchers meetings after losing a little weight with Alli or Xenical. Some people experience side effects of stomach gas, cramping, and diarrhea. Discuss these medications fully with your doctor before trying them.

What can I do about my loss of interest in sex?

Depression is an almost universal drag on sexual interest; it is a kind of anti-aphrodisiac. In the midst of depression, sex seems to move down on the list of life priorities. And as if that weren't bad enough, most modern antidepressants cause problems with sexual function.

Explain to your partner that loss of sexual interest is common in unipolar major depression and that it will return gradually as you become well again. Emphasize that help, understanding, and support are important for your recovery. Caring, insightful partners will understand how depression can cause their significant other to feel distant and will make it clear that depression will not endanger their relationship.

Besides, sex is not the only part of a relationship. This is a time to explore closeness and caring that is not tied to sex. Let your partner know that you want to be held, to be together, and to be intimate without sex for now. You may find new forms of intimacy that both of you will value. Depression can be an opportunity for your relationship to grow despite your negative thoughts and feelings.

If your partner is resistant, pushy, or only interested in his own sexual satisfaction despite your depressive pain, you must explain clearly that you will not engage in sex unless you want to, and that pushiness will only push you farther away.

Is it normal that my sexuality seems to have changed?

As you might expect, most of the information about antidepressants' effects on sexuality has to do with erections and ejaculation, with little attention paid to the problems that antidepressants create for depressed women. For example, SSRIs often make it take so long for women to have an orgasm that sex becomes painful, or it does not seem like it is worth the effort. Some SSRIs like Prozac can even numb the sensitivity of your sexual organs. Generally, it seems that Wellbutrin and Desyrel are the least offensive antidepressants to women's sexuality. The older tricyclic antidepressants elicit surprisingly few complaints about sexual interest and sensitivity. They can sometimes dry the vagina, but most women solve this problem by using a lubricant. Talk to your doctor about your antidepressant side effects, and work with him or her to select a medication and dose that fits your own needs.

Depression has made me feel distant from my partner—should I act on these feelings?

How you feel toward others now is influenced by your depressed thinking. It is not an expression of your most natural self but is rather just a temporary stage you are going through. When you are depressed, it is hard to believe that you are a good, deserving person who can accept love and give love in return. Please wait to make important decisions about your relationship until your depression diminishes—then you will be able to remember how love feels and be able to recognize it within yourself again. You will make a better decision when you are healthy.

It is also important that you refrain from making judgments for others based on what you think is best for them while you are depressed. For example, don't decide to divorce you husband because you think it would be better for him. Let him decide for himself whether he wants to get rid of you and get on with his life, or if he prefers to stay with the woman he loves.

In fact, it is better to avoid making any big decisions about your life while you are depressed, because you are not thinking at full efficiency, and many of your feelings are distorted. If you try to solve major life issues now, you are likely to make bad choices that you will regret later. This is not the best time in your life to marry, divorce, buy or build a house, move to another part of the country, or part company with friends or family. Rather, this is the time for you to work on your medical and psychotherapeutic treatment, lower your stress levels, and develop healthy life habits. Then, when your depression has ebbed, you will be healthier and able to make better decisions than ever.

What do I do if my depressed partner won't get treatment?

Your partner's depression is probably preventing him from seeing the severity of his condition. He may not be able to remember how he felt before he became depressed, and he may assume that depression is his natural state. Some people are not convinced that they have clinical depression until they start feeling normal again. Then they look back at the miserable, lost months (and sometimes years) and regret the needless pain and disappointments they have caused themselves and others.

Unipolar major depression is always unnatural (see Chapters 1 and 2) and needs to be corrected for your spouse to function normally. However, you cannot twist your partner's arm or take him to the doctor at gunpoint. He has to make his own decisions. You can tell him that you care about him and that his condition is causing you pain and unhappiness that could be relieved by a simple doctor's appointment. If you are not sure that you can stay around him if he continues to be depressed, tell him that.

Why has my partner become unreasonably demanding and physical since my depression began?

When a woman becomes depressed, she becomes an easy target for abuse and may get caught up in abusive relationships because of a diminished ability to make good decisions. Numerous women have realized that their partner was unfaithful, a thief, or a scoundrel operating behind their backs once their depression lifted.

You could easily become a target of violent abuse. If violence occurs in your relationship, leave the house immediately. Go to your mother's, sister's, or friend's home, or even go to a women's shelter for the evening. If children are involved, get them out of the house with you.

Find an advocate who can communicate with your partner for you so you will not remain a target for your partner's recriminative abuse. If you wish, you can bring in social service workers or police as protectors and advocates; this is part of their job. In most communities, you can find the telephone numbers for women's shelters and social services in the telephone book.

In addition to being reprehensible and illegal, abuse can keep your depression from healing. If you are unsure whether your relationship is a healthy one, or think that it may be keeping you depressed, it is all right to take some time off. Taking a temporary break from your partner should never endanger the stability of a healthy relationship. Take your time before rushing back into a relationship that may be stressful, injurious, or otherwise detrimental to your health.

Depression can bring out the worst in others, and you have to protect yourself.

My depression increases whenever I look in the mirror—what can I do to feel better about my appearance?

We are born into a culture that has little respect for depressed women. Films, television, and magazines are constantly telling you what you should be like, sending messages that are critical and disheartening if you do not meet artificial cultural standards. Please, do not let this propaganda make your depression worse. Recognize that there is something naturally desirable and beautiful about you, even if your depression is keeping it hidden right now.

Although you do not like yourself now, visualize how you would look if you were feeling great again and going out to parties, picnics, or get-togethers with your family, friends, community, church, and workmates. A smile is the most important thing you can put on, and after you begin receiving support from others, you will feel better about yourself. Going out now and being happier with your looks later is a strategy that works. Staying at home and waiting until you think you look better before you go out does not work.

You should also try to turn your depression around and use it as a motivator to take better care of your health. If you have been putting off exercising, start a sensible exercise schedule, and follow through with it (see Chapter 12, Good Health Habits). You may not feel like exercising, but it's good for your health and can help your depression go away. If you are sleeping poorly, check your sleep hygiene and get better rest. If you have been eating starchy junk foods, get back to a healthy diet again. By the time your depression has lifted, everyone will be able to see your beauty clearly again, including you.

How can I help my depressed friend feel better about herself?

Depression makes people see themselves on the outside like they feel on the inside: worn out and useless. This is why you often see depressed people slump, adopt sad or bitter expressions, develop frown wrinkles in the brow and upper eyelids, and wear drab, shapeless clothing. It's hard to care for yourself during depressed episodes, and depressed women often put up with bad haircuts, ill-fitting clothes, or worn-out shoes.

Help your friend by praising what she is able to do to care for herself. Offer to go with her on shopping trips or to the stylist. See if you can help her find some fun things to do that will help her feel better about herself and remember what she was like before she was depressed.

Where can I find more help on women and depression?

See if you can find any women among your friends, community, or church who have beaten depression, and seek their counsel. Find a local therapy group or support group where you can interact with other depressed women and help each other. Groups on the Internet are less personal, but they can feel more comfortable, especially if you are hesitant or shy. See Appendix A, Resources, for ways to contact other women for mutual support. It can be invaluable to share your troubles and sorrows with someone who's going through the same experiences.

Chapter 15

CRISIS MANAGEMENT AND PREVENTION

- What's the best thing I can do to prevent a depression-related crisis?
- What is the first thing I should do to keep depression crises from happening?
- How can I talk to my depressed loved one when he's so emotional?
- How do I stop playing down my depression in front of my doctor, therapist, and family?
- What, exactly, is my depressed friend going through?
- What do I do if one of the most important people in my life is making my depression worse?
- How can I tell if my loved one's depression is growing worse?
- All I can think about is death—am I crazy?
- What is a "poisonous thought"?
- What can happen if unipolar major depression isn't brought under control?
- Why would someone want to kill himself?
- What can I do to help someone who's contemplating suicide?
- Do suicide hotlines help?
- When should I take a suicide threat seriously?
- Do these terrifying suicidal thoughts mean I'll kill myself?
- What can I hold onto during these suicidal periods?
- Is there anything else I should do to keep from hurting myself?
- Why does my therapist freeze up when I talk about suicide?

What's the best thing I can do to prevent a depression-related crisis?

If you have unipolar major depression and things are getting worse or you are having thoughts of ending your life, you need to have a life plan ready. If you are a family member or friend of a depressed person, you need to know how to provide positive reassurance and head off potential crises without escalating depression or increasing the danger of suicide. You also need to have a life plan ready. In this chapter, you will find options to help you head off severe depression and suicidal tendencies so that you will be better prepared to prevent crises or to deal with them if they happen.

What is the first thing I should do to keep depression crises from happening?

Communication is the most important factor in stopping crises before they begin. If you are depressed, you need to keep your doctor and therapist updated about any changes in your depression, especially if you feel it is getting worse, so they will be prepared to act. If you are having suicidal thoughts, let your doctor and therapist know how frequently they occur and how severe they are. It is up to you to keep others in your life apprised of your condition. Pick a few individuals who can handle this information, and periodically update them so they will not be caught unawares if things begin to go downhill. You want to have a support system already in place in case of trouble.

If you are the friend, spouse, or other family member of the depressed person, you need to establish a line of communication about her depression. It is your responsibility to offer to talk about her feelings and to let her know that you will be there to support her if she needs you. If you are a close family member or significant other of the depressed individual, you may want to identify yourself to her doctor and therapist. This just consists of picking up the telephone, introducing yourself, and letting them know that they can call if you can ever help with your loved one's depression. This also opens communication with the doctor and therapist so that if you ever need to call *them* about a potential problem, they will know who you are and recognize you as their ally.

If you are having difficulty understanding your loved one's depression, you may consider asking the doctor and therapist to help. You may offer to pay for their time or schedule an appointment so they can talk with you, answer your questions, and give you suggestions about what you can say and do. Do not expect to learn specifics about the depressed person's condition or treatment, because this is privileged information.

How can I talk to my depressed loved one when he's so emotional?

Here are some suggestions to help you discuss and empathize with your loved one's pain.

- Do be willing to listen quietly and patiently without injecting your own comments, observations, or advice. Allow your loved one to express his sad and angry feelings openly without interference.
- Don't be frustrated, argumentative, or angry with him. The enemy here is the depression, not the person who is depressed.
- Do let him know that you care about him, and express the honest hope and confidence that he *will* find solutions to his problems.
- Don't try to fix his depression by yourself. Instead, concentrate on being the best friend, parent, or spouse that you can be.
- Do refer him back to his doctor and therapist for any clinical questions or problems.

- Don't ever be sworn to secrecy or agree to become an intermediary between your loved one and his doctor, therapist, employer, spouse, family, or anyone else.
- Do be open and honest in your communication. Your loved one needs to know that he can trust your feedback.
- Don't close your eyes at the mention of death or suicide. Simply let your loved one know that you care about him and that you would miss him if he were gone.

How do I stop playing down my depression in front of my doctor, therapist, and family?

Try to open up to your doctor and therapist and get them to understand how serious things are for you now. If they do not hear your need, then try discussing the Emotion Checklist on page 250 with them to improve your emotional communication. Try to open up a new dialog with your friends and family and help them understand how you are really feeling and what they can do to help. Explain that you could not share the full extent of your depression problem before but you are willing to talk about it now if they are interested. Remember, they do want to help you, but you have to let them.

What, exactly, is my depressed friend going through?

Depression is different from a bad mood. Unipolar major depression is caused by abnormalities in brain cells, thought patterns, and behavioral habits that have deep and powerful influences on how your friend is experiencing her life. For example, when you are suffering from unipolar major depression, even happy events cannot cheer you up. When depression becomes severe, every positive experience seems like an exception and every negative experience proves the point that your life is falling apart and your situation is hopeless. Your friend's depressed mind may be clouded and its contents unclear and scary, almost as if she were being forced to watch a horror movie.

Even after you have heard this, it still may not be possible to understand the experience of unipolar major depression unless you have been through it. Concentrate on being a good listener, and let your friend teach you about her depression.

What do I do if one of the most important people in my life is making my depression worse?

Occasionally, a friend or family member will deny that you are suffering from depression, despite all evidence to the contrary. They are hoping that if they just close their eyes, this depression business will suddenly go away and you will be the same as you were before. This approach may work for ostriches, but not for humans. Be patient with these individuals; they are struggling with issues of their own. If you have to, cut them out of their life until either they accept your depression or you are healthy enough to handle them.

How can I tell if my loved one's depression is growing worse?

The best way is just to ask her if things are getting worse. If she is suffering significantly more than she did before, you should be concerned.

It may be hard for your loved one to be objective about her condition. If she is in denial, she may try to explain away her depression by blaming it on bad luck, life disappointments, or other people, including you. She may tell you that she is just having a normal reaction to bad circumstances and that she has to suffer with her negative thoughts and emotions. However, there is no normal human response that leads to isolation, obsession, incapacity, or suicidality, and there is no excuse for letting someone with unipolar major depression suffer unnecessarily.

If you need more clues to the severity of your loved one's depression, see if she has lost interest in the activities of her life. Find out if she is refusing to take advantage of supportive resources like her doctor and therapist. Be concerned if she seems to have intrusive thoughts, decreased speech, impaired logic, or confusion. Here are some other signs of worsening unipolar major depression:

- Aloofness and detachment from family and friends
- Preoccupation with death and dying
- Spending too much time alone
- Losing interest in work, school, or home responsibilities
- Increasing frequency of accidents or unnecessary risk-taking
- Increasing use of alcohol or drugs
- Poor hygiene, including failing to bathe, brush teeth, or wear clean clothes.
- Decreasing appetite or sleep

All I can think about is death—am I crazy?

People with severe depression often find themselves thinking about death. Thoughts about your death or the death of others, and the topic of death in general, may pop up in your mind out of nowhere. Television and movies, even comedies, can start you thinking about your brief mortality and ultimate demise.

This is not unusual, and it certainly does not mean that you're crazy; however, you do not gain anything by lingering on these thoughts. In fact, you should use stress-reduction techniques, therapy, and medication to wash them from your mind altogether.

What is a "poisonous thought"?

"Poisonous thoughts" are what we call the negative thoughts and memories that can throw someone immediately into depression.

Usually these are memories that have become very charged with sad and hopeless emotions. Poisonous thoughts usually occur in individuals who are in the middle of or recovering from severe depression. If a depressed friend or family member asks you earnestly not to mention a particularly emotionally charged memory, it is a good idea to avoid bringing it up until the depression episode has waned.

What can happen if unipolar major depression isn't brought under control?

The worst outcome from unipolar major depression is death. According to the Johns Hopkins Hospital website, an unbelievable 15 percent of people with severe depression kill themselves. Think about it this way. If you were in an emergency room sitting next to six other severely depressed individuals, one of you would end up taking your own life. You do not want this to happen to you or anyone you care about.

Most unipolar major depression is undiagnosed, and most suicides are unreported, so the true number of suicides is probably a lot higher. Many more deaths from supposed automobile and pedestrian accidents, drowning, fatal falls, and so forth, are really suicides without warning, explanation, or suicide notes.

Why would someone want to kill himself?

The pain experienced in unipolar major depression may be greater than in any other illness. Even patients with bone cancer and other terribly painful illnesses do not usually kill themselves to get relief, unless they are also suffering from unipolar major depression. Some depressed individuals who do not really want to die end up killing themselves in fits of despair, impulsivity, or poor judgment.

If you are seriously depressed, you must take the danger of possible suicide seriously. If you are close to a depressed person, it is often a good idea to ask about suicide. More often than not, the depressed person will be glad to get the secret off his or her chest.

What can I do to help someone who's contemplating suicide?

The best kind of help you can provide is to tell her that you love her and you are sorry she's in so much pain. Tell her that you would miss her dearly if she were no longer in your life. Tell her that you wish that you could make her feel better right now, but she will just have to wait a little longer.

Most people who have been moderately depressed have considered the reprieve that suicide promises, and they are usually relieved to find out that others know how common suicidal thoughts are in unipolar major depression. Even if your loved one is not open to discussing her feelings now, you will have opened a pathway for communications that she can use if her suicidal thoughts and impulses escalate in the future.

You do not have to mention suicide by name if you are uncomfortable talking about it. If you are comfortable discussing suicide, do so with calm caring. It is okay to tell depressed people that you hope they do not kill themselves.

Do suicide hotlines help?

Suicide hotlines can save lives. *The Journal of the American Medical Association* (*JAMA*) website recommends the National Suicide Prevention Lifeline: 1-800-273-8255. You can usually find local emergency suicide numbers in the front of your telephone book (sources for other local, state, and national hotlines and suicide services are listed in Appendix A, Resources). Here's a list of reasons to call a hotline:

- If you feel you might be in danger of hurting yourself
- If your doctor and therapist are unavailable
- To get referrals for doctors and therapists if you do not have one
- If you are concerned that someone else may be in danger

Unfortunately, hotlines cannot come into your home and take the pills from your hand. If you are in danger of killing yourself, have a responsible friend or family member stay with you. They should be close enough to see and hear you, and prepared to talk or just sit quietly. Just the presence of someone who cares is a reminder of why you keep on living.

When should I take a suicide threat seriously?

There's no way to tell if suicide threats will be acted on; sometimes the depressed person does not even know himself. There is no reliable way to predict suicide in advance. Therefore, all suicide threats must be taken seriously.

Find someone to stay with your suicidal loved one, and call his doctor and therapist. Intoxication from alcohol or illicit drugs greatly increases his risk of doing something impulsive, so it is best to take both away if possible. Take away guns and knives, and flush away any old, unused pills that could be used in a suicide attempt.

Some situations increase the risk of someone killing himself: If your loved one has attempted suicide before, the odds are greater that he will try again. If he has planned the way he intends to kill himself, then he is at higher risk of suicide, and if he is raging, panicking, irrational, illogical, hysterical, or paranoid, he may act without thinking. If your loved one is all alone, loneliness and lack of support can make it seem that no one cares what happens to him.

Some Suicide Warning Signs
- Stops being sad and starts to act nonchalant, uncaring, resigned, or distant
- Suddenly becomes quiet, secretive, or guarded
- Stops talking about getting well
- Begins to talk about how things would be without her
- Starts giving away prized possessions
- Seems to be saying good-bye to family and friends
- Collects pills, acquires a weapon, or talks about a place where suicide could take place
- Suddenly begins to make a will or final arrangements for death

Do these terrifying suicidal thoughts mean I'll kill myself?

Fortunately, you are already different from most people who commit suicide. The fact that you are reading this book shows that you are working to reduce your depression. As long as you are resisting depression, you have hope. If you have been following this book, you already have a doctor and therapist or are about to get professional help. Active participation in your medical and psychotherapeutic treatment greatly reduces your risk from suicide.

Remember that thinking about suicide is vastly different from killing yourself. If you really wanted to kill yourself, you would be dead already, not here reading this book about how to end your depression. It is vitally important that you let your doctor and therapist know that you are thinking about suicide, so they can help you. When you tell your doctor and therapist that you are having thoughts of suicide, make sure you explain their frequency and severity. Here is a checklist that can help you identify and track your suicidal thoughts.

SUICIDE SEVERITY CHECKLIST

This list will help you clarify your condition to yourself, your doctor, and your therapist, as well as help you track your dangerous thoughts over time.

Check the box that best describes your current situation:

DATE: ___ / ___ / ___	Never	A Few Times a Month	A Few Times a Week	Almost Every Day	Many Times a Day
Thoughts of suicide	❏	❏	❏	❏	❏
Thinking about how to do it	❏	❏	❏	❏	❏
Visualizing it happening	❏	❏	❏	❏	❏
Deciding to do it sometime	❏	❏	❏	❏	❏
Preparing to do it	❏	❏	❏	❏	❏
Setting a date to do it	❏	❏	❏	❏	❏
Attempting suicide	❏	❏	❏	❏	❏

What can I hold onto during these suicidal periods?

All humans have an innate quality of hopefulness. Some part of you wants you to stay alive—perhaps every part. Look inside yourself to find the reasons you have *not* killed yourself. Some people believe that killing is contrary to their religion, and suicide is like murdering themselves. Others say they are afraid they'll botch the job and leave themselves crippled and in pain. Most say they do not want to bring grief to their parents or leave their spouse, children, friends, or pets alone. Some even say they do not want to cause pain to their doctor and therapist. There is something slightly selfish and narcissistic about killing oneself that is abhorrent to many people, despite the pain they are experiencing.

If you are experiencing suicidal thoughts, you should at least let your doctor and therapist have a chance at improving your mood. If you are only doing psychotherapy, consider adding medications that may work more quickly. If you are only taking medications, begin psychotherapy and discuss your suicidal thoughts and feelings calmly, logically, objectively, and in detail with your therapist.

If you feel suicidal, please give yourself the opportunity to change your mind. Remember, your need to escape is based on the assumption that your life will not get any better. It may seem like your happiness is far away, but even a small improvement in your life experience will feel heartening and liberating now. It is hard to make good decisions when you are depressed, so it's best not to make any decision as important as ending your life until you are feeling more like yourself. It's safe to say that depressed people who changed their minds about suicide have all been glad that they did when they began to recover.

Even if it seems like you cannot get better, depression *can* be healed. Keep putting suicide off until you feel better, and you will be glad that you did.

Is there anything else I should do to keep from hurting myself?

Distance yourself from any means of suicide. If you are thinking of taking an overdose, give your medicine to someone who can hold it and give you a day's worth at a time. If you have thoughts of jumping from the roof of a building, stay away from that roof while you are still depressed. Do not use alcohol or drugs that could make you act without thinking.

Remove all possible weapons from your home. For example, if you are thinking of cutting yourself, take away any sharp knives until your depression has abated. It is better to use a butter knife to cut your steak than use a steak knife to cut yourself.

Most importantly, make use of your support system. Call and see your doctor and therapist when the situation seems dangerous. Recruit your family and friends to spend time with you when you are afraid of hurting yourself. Make it difficult or impossible for you to kill yourself on a whim.

Why does my therapist freeze up when I talk about suicide?

It appears that your therapist is willing to take your suicidal thoughts seriously, which is good. However, it is important for you to be able to discuss your suicidal feelings and intentions comfortably, objectively, and in detail with your therapist.

Usually experienced psychiatrists and professional psychotherapists have worked through their own fear of death in the course of their own psychotherapy or analysis. Some less experienced doctors and psychotherapists are still terrified that they might be responsible for the death of one of their patients if they intervene. This fear makes it difficult for them to help you, especially in a crisis. If your doctor or psychotherapist is not comfortable discussing your suicidal thoughts and emotions, you may have to begin looking for someone who is.

Chapter 16

WHEN ALL ELSE FAILS

- How do I know when it is time to take someone to the hospital?
- What can the hospital do to prevent my friend from killing himself?
- What's the best way to help my loved one get admitted into the hospital quickly?
- Is there any way to speed up the time we spend in the emergency room?
- What can the hospital do to help with my depression?
- Why is the psychiatric ward so stark?
- What can I do to prepare for my loved one's release from the hospital?
- What is "psychotic depression"?
- What types of hallucinations are common?
- Can discussing my loved one's hallucinations help her in any way?
- How long should I wait for my treatment to work?
- What are some common causes of treatment failure?
- What should I do if psychotherapy or medication doesn't help me?
- After a year of extensive treatment, my depression is still bad—what next?
- At what point do I decide that nothing is going to make me any better?

How do I know when it is time to take someone to the hospital?

That's easy: If you start wondering whether it is time for someone to go to the hospital, then it is time for him to go.

If it seems that he is in danger of hurting himself or anyone else in any way, he needs to go to the hospital immediately. This is not a negotiable situation; he *must* be hospitalized right away where no harm can come to him or those around him. If you cannot get through to his doctor in time, call 911. When the emergency medical technicians arrive, clearly explain that there is a danger that he will harm himself or someone else. If the EMT personnel concur that a danger exists, they can take him to the hospital, where he will be evaluated by hospital doctors.

What can the hospital do to prevent my friend from killing himself?

The best thing that the hospital can do to prevent imminent suicide is to put your friend on constant watch, first in the emergency room and then on the hospital psychiatry ward. The surest way to prevent someone from killing herself is for someone else to be there to prevent it. The nurses and the technicians have experience in keeping depressed people from harming themselves, and they'll be following explicit hospital guidelines on what to do in a suicide emergency.

In addition to staying with and watching your friend, the hospital can provide an environment free of deadly objects, treat her depression, and offer sedation if she is panicky or afraid.

What's the best way to help my loved one get admitted into the hospital quickly?

If your loved one's depression is getting so severe that you fear for his welfare, call his doctor and tell her what you think. If you think that hospitalization is a good idea, say so. If she agrees, the doctor may be able to arrange for your loved one to be preadmitted to the hospital. With preadmission, when you arrive, there will be someone waiting to take your loved one right up to a room on the psychiatric ward. Without it, however, you may have to bring your sleeping bags to the emergency room.

Is there any way to speed up the time we spend in the emergency room?

The hospital admission process can be like trying to find your way through the Minotaur's labyrinth. The most time-consuming part of the process is waiting in the emergency room. If the patient's doctor is not available or unable to arrange preadmission, try your primary care doctor, or any doctor you know, to see if they can call the hospital and streamline the admission. Usually, calling 911 or an ambulance is faster than taking the depressed person to the hospital on your own. In fact, when patients come in on their own, they may be pushed right back out the door again if the danger to themselves or others is not immediately apparent.

What can the hospital do to help with my depression?

The hospital can provide experienced personnel who are available around the clock to care for your depression, consult with hospital psychiatrists and psychotherapists who can provide second opinions, and perform a medical assessment to make sure that no internal medical problems are complicating your depression. If your medications need to be changed, they can often be adjusted faster in the hospital environment, where there is plenty of professional support available.

In the hospital, you may also have access to special services provided to patients on the hospital psychiatric ward. These may include individual psychotherapy, group psychotherapy (run by nurses, psychotherapists, or clinicians-in-training), occupational therapy, art therapy, music therapy, visualization exercises, and relaxation techniques. These in-house programs vary widely in availability and quality from hospital to hospital. Group psychotherapy is usually what helps patients the most. The opportunity to get the support of other people who are depressed can often be enlightening. You will find out that you are not alone in your suffering, and supportive relationships made in the hospital are often maintained for years afterward. Skillful group leaders can use the group to improve insight into your depression and hasten the progress of your treatment.

Why is the psychiatric ward so stark?

Unfortunately, many patients abhor the hospital experience, especially if they went there involuntarily. The institution of hospitals is, well, institutional. Unless you are paying an arm and a leg, there will not be Chippendale furniture on the floor or Degas on the walls. The furnishings are spare, and any objects that could be used to cause injury have been removed. Some patients take umbrage at being housed with other patients who are "mentally ill," but this may be a potent eye-opener to people in denial of the severity of their depression. If you have complaints, remember that hospitalization is not meant to be a rest cure or a vacation resort; its purpose is to keep people alive and speed up their recovery.

What can I do to prepare for my loved one's release from the hospital?

Toward the end of her hospital stay, hospital discharge planners should make arrangements for your loved one to leave the hospital with medication in hand and an appointment for follow-up with a doctor in the next few days. If you like, you can call the hospital before her release and ask them about their "discharge plan" to make sure they have one that will work.

What is "psychotic depression"?

Psychotic unipolar major depression affects approximately three million people annually in the United States. Because psychotic individuals cannot distinguish reality from fantasy, their behavior is unpredictable, and we cannot accurately assess their safety. For example, people with psychotic depression are approximately seventy times more likely to commit suicide than the general population. Hospitalization is the safest form of treatment until the psychosis is brought under control.

Psychotic depression is the most severe state of unipolar major depression, where people experience and believe in the existence of things that are not evident to other people. Usually when doctors speak of psychosis, they are referring to the experience of delusions and hallucinations. Depressive delusions are sad and negative beliefs that are not evident to other people. They are intense fantasies that have their roots in the intrusive thoughts and negative distortions common to depression. For example, people with psychotic depression whose aches, pains, and doubts are magnified by their mental illness might begin to believe they are suffering from cancer. A person's mild jealousy can grow into the delusion that his spouse is having an affair with her employer. Delusions can be nihilistic (a belief that you are doomed), deprecatory (a belief that you are guilty or bad), or persecutory (a belief that others wish you ill or intend to harm you).

Hallucinations most commonly take the form of hearing noises or voices inside one's head, called auditory hallucinations. Sometimes the voices sound like vague conversations in the background or voices arguing, describing what you are doing, or telling you what to do. Some patients hear their parents arguing inside their heads.

Less common are visual hallucinations, where you see things that are not there. Visual hallucinations can be dramatic and scary, like watching the tips of your fingers, hand, wrist, and arm gradually vanish into thin air. The experience of looking through horrible scenes of death and destruction superimposed over your normal field of view has been called "horror movie hallucinations."

What types of hallucinations are common?

The experiences that other people, billboards, the radio, or television are talking about you or directly to you are called ideas of reference. One of the scariest experiences in psychosis is to be watching television and see one of the television characters turn, look you straight in the eyes, and speak directly to you about personal topics. Knowing that other depressed people experience hallucinations can help make it a little less scary if it happens to you.

If you are suffering from this extreme form of major depression, you are in need of immediate attention. When you are unable to differentiate fantasy from reality, you have the potential to make dangerous decisions, be taken advantage of by others, or even impulsively commit suicide.

Can discussing my loved one's hallucinations help her in any way?

There is sometimes a tendency to become fascinated by the weird world of psychosis, and plenty of time can be wasted thinking about and analyzing the possible meanings of delusions and hallucinations. Sometimes family and friends talk at length with the psychotic individual about their strange perceptions. Unfortunately, there is little to be gained in studying the content of hallucinations. Psychotic disturbances are a sign that the depressed person is extremely sick and needs to be cared for; that's all.

How long should I wait for my treatment to work?

The accepted wisdom is that you should wait five weeks at the highest recommended dose before giving up on an antidepressant. Psychotherapy should probably show some benefit within four to eight weeks.

Sometimes it helps to see your doctor and therapist more frequently if your depression is severe or not responding to treatment. This maximizes your access to treatment, and it also gives them a better opportunity to observe your progress. Often, your doctor and therapist can see signs of improvement or deterioration before they are evident to you.

Overall, you and your doctor and therapist should all be able to see some clear, noticeable improvements within two months of starting treatment.

What are some common causes of treatment failure?

By far, the most common cause of medication failure is taking too low a dose for too short a time. For example, depressed individuals may be taking only one-half to one-tenth of the maximum recommended dose of their antidepressant. Others believe that an antidepressant trial had failed when they have only taken the antidepressant for a few days. If you have been taking one of the antidepressants in this book at the maximum recommended dose for four to six weeks without any results, then it is time to change your medication strategy. Look at the charts and descriptions in chapters 5, 6, and 7, and change antidepressants, add another antidepressant, or add another medication as an adjuvant. Do not give up until you have followed your new plan for four to six weeks.

The most common cause of psychotherapy failure is not seeing the therapist frequently enough. If you only see your therapist once or twice a month, then you are not doing enough therapy to quell serious unipolar major depression. Try changing to once or twice per week until your depression begins to respond.

The next most common cause of therapy ineffectiveness is the failure to employ a type of psychotherapy that is specifically designed to treat depression (see Chapter 10, Choosing between Psychotherapies). For example, if your therapist acts like your best friend or just tells you everything is okay and not to worry, it is not going to help your depression.

What should I do if psychotherapy or medication doesn't help me?

The simplest thing you can do to increase the effectiveness of your treatment is to get both medication and psychotherapeutic treatment at the same time, if you are not already doing so. Participation in both types of treatment will usually speed up your progress as well.

Also, failing to reduce stress frequently holds back depressed individuals from full recovery. Even the best medications and psychotherapy may not be enough if you continue to work twelve hours per day, stay in a damaging relationship, or persist in impulsive and addictive behaviors. It is common for depressed individuals to take on more stress in their lives as soon as their depression starts to go away. As you can imagine, this is sufficient to torpedo any treatment progress. Try reducing your life stresses, and take advantage of the relaxation exercises in Chapter 13 (Stress-Reduction Techniques).

After a year of extensive treatment, my depression is still bad—what next?

The importance of finding a doctor and therapist that possess a good education, good clinical training, and plenty of experience and success treating unipolar major depression cannot be stressed enough. Sometimes this is not good enough, and you need to get a second opinion. You should try to get a second opinion from a psychiatrist, especially if you have been seeing an internist, obstetrician/gynecologist, or family doctor for depression treatment. See Chapter 8, Finding a Doctor, for help in finding a consulting psychiatrist for a second opinion. You should be prepared to explain the details of your depression history as well as your medication and psychotherapy treatment, beginning from the first moment you realized that you might be depressed. Also, it is a good idea to bring test results and past medical records.

After your consultant tells you his opinion, ask plenty of questions until you understand everything he is saying. You may want to discuss your consultant's opinion with your current doctor and therapist. Remember that you and your doctor are still a team as long as you remain their patient, and you are still entitled to their opinions and support.

If it seems that your current doctor and therapist are just not up to the job, it is time for new blood. Go back to the section on finding a doctor, and try again. If you liked the conclusions of the consulting doctor and felt comfortable in his presence, you can ask if he will take over your case or suggest another doctor who thinks the same way he does.

At what point do I decide that nothing is going to make me any better?

Unipolar major depression makes it seem that you cannot escape the prison of your thoughts and feelings. However, people overcome the most severe depression, and you can too. Believe in yourself, fight hard, and good luck! Remember that unipolar major depression is only beyond hope if you give up.

Here are some tips for success in your fight against depression:

- Recognize that unipolar major depression is a serious but treatable clinical disorder.
- Recognize that unipolar major depression is a disease of the nervous system, not the product of bad luck, weak will, personality flaws, past sins, or personal inadequacy.
- Get evaluated by a psychiatrist or other experienced doctor to see if you have a diagnosis of unipolar major depression. Get a physical examination to rule out covert internal disease.
- Form an alliance with a good doctor and therapist to provide antidepressant therapy, appropriate psychotherapy, or better yet, both. Use the self-therapy programs presented in Appendix D of this book.
- Develop healthy habits of nutrition, sleep, and exercise. Avoid the use of alcohol, tobacco, marijuana, or addicting stimulants.
- Learn and use stress-reduction and meditation techniques to minimize the damaging effects of stress on yourself, your life, and your health.
- Use your social support system, take part in outside activities, and follow your faith.
- Be prepared in advance for crises, and know what to do to prevent or stop suicidal tendencies.

Epilogue

Sometimes we live no particular way but our own.
Sometimes we visit the country and live in your home.
Sometimes we ride your wild horses,
Sometimes we walk alone.
Sometimes the songs that we hear are just songs of our own.

Appendix A RESOURCES

Can you treat your depression over the Internet? Probably not, but there are many resources to help you along your way. Here are websites recommended by patients and their families and suggested by doctors. They are constantly changing, so check the information you read with your doctor and therapist before accepting that it is true. Be especially wary of sites that have an ax to grind, are selling anything, or ask for your money. With that said, go ahead and dive in!

Professional Service Organizations

Doctors' associations have a wealth of the newest information, and you can have access to much of it via their websites. Search these sites to find out the credentials of doctors and therapists, the newest medications, the rationale behind different types of psychotherapy, and other useful tidbits of information.

The Academy of Cognitive Therapy

An association of cognitive therapists that follow the teachings of the psychotherapist leader Aaron Beck, MD. They also will provide you a referral to a cognitive therapist.

www.academyofct.org

The American Association of Family Physicians
Family physicians are educated in the recognition and treatment of depression, and their website has useful information on what family doctors do.
www.aafp.org
www.aafp.org/afp/20060101/83.html

The American Medical Association (AMA)
This is the major organization representing all types of physicians in the United States. They offer information for doctors and patients and publish the *Journal of the American Medical Association (JAMA)* and the professional psychiatric journal called *Archives of Psychiatry*.
www.ama-assn.org

The American Psychiatric Association (APA)
The APA is the premier professional psychiatric society in the United States. Their website provides information on psychiatric illnesses and treatment, current news, interest groups, advocacy, and ethics. They publish the *Journal of the American Psychiatric Association*.
www.psych.org

The American Psychoanalytic Association (APsaA)
This website will answer some of your questions about psychoanalysis.
www.apsa.org

The American Psychological Association (APA)
Called the "big APA" because there are so many more psychologists than psychiatrists in this country, the American Psychological Association is a vast organization with many services and viewpoints. They provide books, journal articles, and research findings

on depression and other topics. You can also use the site to find psychologists who practice in your area, as well as a list of psychological associations and related organizations around the world.
www.apa.org

The Association for Behavioral and Cognitive Therapies

This organization supports and provides referrals to behavioral and cognitive therapists.
www.abct.org

The International Society for Interpersonal Psychotherapy

This site for interpersonal psychotherapists explains what they do and how their techniques work to heal depression.
www.interpersonalpsychotherapy.org

The National Association of Cognitive Behavioral Therapists

This is a website for cognitive behavioral therapists. They also have information on Dr. Albert Ellis's groundbreaking Rational Emotive Therapy.
www.nacbt.org

The Natural Medicines Comprehensive Database

This website is the premiere resource on the medicine and pharmacology of vitamins, supplements, and herbal products. It is searchable and updated daily, but it is also very expensive to use. Maybe your doctor will subscribe and let you use it. There is also a consumer website at the address below.
www.naturaldatabase.com

The World Psychiatric Association

This psychiatric society provides international information for professionals and the public. The site contains a useful listing of hospitals, psychiatry departments, and mental health organizations around the world.

www.wpanet.org

Government Services

These federal websites contain a huge amount of accurate, useful information, including publications about unipolar major depression, news about medications and clinical trials, access to medical articles and research, and links to local groups and resources.

ClinicalTrials.gov

This is the official place to learn about new treatments for unipolar major depression. It lists federally and privately supported research studies into new medications and nonmedication treatments for depression. Just type "depression" in the search box, and you will find out about investigations taking place all over the country. Or you can search the new antidepressants mentioned in this book and find out their progress through the stages of testing and licensure.

www.clinicaltrials.gov

Medline Plus

This site from the National Institutes of Health and the National Library of Medicine has a database with information about thousands of prescription and over-the-counter medications.

http://medlineplus.gov
www.nlm.nih.gov/medlineplus

National Strategy for Suicide Prevention

This site has lots of information on suicide prevention, plus a national policy aimed at eliminating suicide in this country. It is a service of the Federal Substance Abuse and Mental Health Service Administration (SAMHSA).

www.mentalhealth.samhsa.gov/suicideprevention

National Institute of Mental Health (NIMH)

This organization distributes information on mental health and mental health research as well as offering public meetings, advocacy, and access to legislation on mental health issues. This is the real thing.

www.nimh.nih.gov

www.nimh.nih.gov/health/publications/depression/complete-publication.shtml

NIMH Psychoactive Drug Screening Program (PDSP) Database

Although it is quite complex, this may be the most remarkable resource on the Web. Here you can find out how every medication works inside the brain. Try picking a medication and entering a value of 1000 in the box labeled K_i .It is the brainchild of Professor Bryan Roth, MD, PhD, Department of Pharmacology, University of North Carolina, Chapel Hill, NC.

http://kidb.bioc.cwru.edu/pdsp.php

National Institute on Drug Abuse (NIDA)

This website shares information and research on drug abuse and addiction from the major government agency devoted to the topic.

www.nida.nih.gov

Substance Abuse and Mental Health Service Administration (SAMHSA)

SAMHSA's National Mental Health Information Center provides a wealth of online mental health information and resources, including a tool that allows you to locate mental health services in your area as well as a list of national toll-free hotlines that provide mental health resources and referrals.

www.mentalhealth.samhsa.gov

U.S. Food and Drug Administration

Their Center for Food Safety and Applied Nutrition has a wealth of information about keeping healthy. Look for their Food Labeling Guide that tells you what all the claims on food labels really mean.

www.cfsan.fda.gov

www.cfsan.fda.gov/~dms/flg-6c.html

Information, Advocacy, and Support Groups

These public and private organizations span a broad range of services, but they are all working hard to help unipolar major depression sufferers. These websites can be the starting point to find support groups, join national organizations, subscribe to newsletters, locate conventions, and to enter the politics of health care.

The American Foundation for Suicide Prevention (AFSP)

The AFSP funds research, education, and programs to treat depression and prevent suicide. The website provides suicide facts, danger signals, and advice on what to do if a loved one may be contemplating suicide. Topics include information on suicide research, meetings, events, and survivor support groups in your area.

www.afsp.org

The American Psychiatric Association Alliance

This division of the American Psychiatric Association is dedicated to patients' needs.

www.apaalliance.org

Befrienders Worldwide

An international organization that offers help lines for different countries and provides support, information, and opportunities to help others.

www.befrienders.org
www.befrienders.org/helplines/helplines.asp?c2=USA

Cbel.com

An index to many professional organizations, articles, private web pages, and even mailing lists on unipolar major depression.

www.cbel.com/mood_disorders

Depression and Bipolar Support Alliance

Formerly the National Association for Depression and Manic Depression (NADMD), this organization provides information on advocacy, communication with lawmakers, speakers, support groups, discussion, chat, and an opportunity to share your personal story. They publish a newsletter called *Outreach*.

www.dbsalliance.org

Emotions Anonymous

Emotions Anonymous is a twelve-step organization similar to Alcoholics Anonymous. Participants meet regularly to work toward recovery from emotional difficulties. Their diverse membership includes people of every age, socioeconomic status, and educational background.

www.emotionsanonymous.org

Families for Depression Awareness

This group's mission is to help families recognize and manage depression. It also seeks to reduce the stigma associated with depressive disorders and help families cope with depression.
www.familyaware.org/depression/default.php

International Association for Suicide Prevention

This is a multilingual website run by a private organization that organizes volunteers and information to help prevent suicide. It has an association with the World Health Organization.
www.med.uio.no/iasp

Johns Hopkins Hospital and Health System

This is a site promoting the doctors and services of Johns Hopkins Hospital. It also contains information on unipolar major depression, general health, and access to health-related newsletters and other publications.
www.hopkinsmedicine.org/Psychiatry
www.hopkinsmedicine.org/Psychiatry/publications

Journal of the American Medical Association Patient Pages

The website of the biggest medical journal in the world contains lots of information for patients.
http://jama.ama-assn.org
http://jama.ama-assn.org/cgi/collection/depression
http://jama.ama-assn.org/cgi/content/full/293/20/2558

Mayo Clinic

The website of this famous clinic offers information on the nature and causes of unipolar major depression, and options for treating it.
www.mayoclinic.com

Mental Health America (*MHA*)

Formerly known as the National Mental Health Association, MHA is a nonprofit organization offering advocacy, education, research, and support for many mental and emotional illnesses. It includes information on health care reform and health consumers' rights, including parity of mental health benefits with other health coverage.
www.mentalhealthamerica.net

National Alliance on Mental Illness (*NAMI*)

NAMI is a grassroots advocacy, support, and self-help organization for people with mental illnesses, their families, and their friends. The website offers information about mental illness with a special focus on schizophrenia and other psychotic disorders, government policy and legislation, legal issues and patients' rights, treatment breakthroughs, programs, support groups, and a helpline.
www.nami.org

National Mental Health Information Center

This site features information on advocacy, press releases, and access to information from national publications and libraries.
www.mentalhealth.org

National Suicide Prevention Lifeline

The *Journal of the American Medical Association* recommends calling this site's hotline at 1-800-273-8255 for immediate help if you or someone you know is in danger of suicide.
www.suicidepreventionlifeline.org

National Suicide Hotlines

This website, which is linked to Suicide.com, gives the numbers of hotlines in each state so you can find one near you, as well as links to information and opinion aimed at keeping you alive.
http://suicidehotlines.com
http://suicidehotlines.com/national.html

National Women's Health Resource Center

The National Women's Health Resource Center site contains excellent overviews of depression and other health topics of interest to women.
www.healthywomen.org

Natural Medicines Comprehensive Database

This website contains a searchable database that has all the latest recommendations and research on vitamins, supplements, and herbal extracts. It comes from the editors of the giant reference book of the same name. It is too bad that they charge a lot to let you use the database, because it is great. Maybe you can get a subscription as a present from a wealthy relative.
www.naturaldatabase.com

PDR Health

This website by the people at Thompson Healthcare (publishers of the *Physicians' Desk Reference*) provides consumers with plain-English information on the safe and effective use of prescription and nonprescription drugs.
www.pdrhealth.com

Recovery International

This is a mental health self-help program based on the work of Dr. Abraham W. Low. Dr. Low believed that depressed

individuals could learn to control their responses to life stressors and internal thoughts.
www.recovery-inc.com

Suicide Awareness Voices of Education (SAVE)
SAVE is an organization dedicated to the prevention of suicide. They offer a newsletter, *Voices of SAVE*, information, events, and products in an easy-to-access format.
www.save.org

Support Partners and Support Partners: Canine Companions
The site, sponsored by the Eli Lilly pharmaceutical company, offers educational material about depression, suggestions for other online resources, and tips for people who are caring for someone with depression. The information on how to integrate your dog into your depression support system is wonderful.
www.supportpartnersprogram.com

WebMD
This site includes a comprehensive and easy-to-follow overview of depression, its symptoms, causes, treatments, and more.
www.webmd.com

Wikipedia on Assertiveness
This Wikipedia site explains the techniques of assertiveness training that can give you an edge in negotiating with your insurance company, employer, family, doctor, and therapist. Most of the techniques are found in the book by Manuel Juan Smith called *When I Say No, I Feel Guilty* (Bantam Books, 1985).
http://en.wikipedia.org/wiki/Assertiveness

Private Depression Websites

These websites contain opinions and help offered by individuals and private groups.

Dr. Wes Burgess's Website

In addition to describing my practice, my website contains professional medical articles, excerpts from my books, and notes on a variety of mental health issues including unipolar major depression. **www.wesburgess.yourMD.com**

Depression Fallout

This is a message board where family members of depressed individuals can talk to one another. **www.depressionfallout.com**

Dr. Ivan Goldberg's Depression Central

Dr. Goldberg has much to say on the topic of depression and other mental illnesses. **www.psycom.net/depression.central.html**

Find the Light

This website offers peer support groups that meet over the Internet. **www.findthelight.net**

Health Central—My Depression Connection

This site contains a lot of discussion, by doctors and patients with unipolar major depression, as well as a list of recent publications on depression. **www.healthcentral.com/depression**

McMan's Depression and Bipolar Web
This website by John McManamy airs much information on unipolar major depression and bipolar depression.
www.mcmanweb.com

Mood Garden
Mood Garden is a pleasant site with message board, forums, blogs, and depression information.
www.moodgarden.com

Psych Central
Psych Central provides a mixed bag of information, advertisements, and useful chat.
www.psychcentral.com

Professional Books on Unipolar Major Depression and Medical Science
You can find some of the same reference books that doctors use in university libraries, medical school bookstores, and online. These books are usually expensive, heavy, and so full of medical jargon that they are quite difficult to read, but they contain answers you cannot find anywhere else. Here are some from my bookcase:

Mark Beers and Robert Brew, editors. *The Merck Manual of Diagnosis and Therapy*. John Wiley & Sons, 1999.

> *The Merck Manual* is a reasonably priced medical text with information on all medical conditions for doctors and other medical professionals.

Mark H. Beers, editor. *The Merck Manual of Medical Information.* Simon & Schuster, 2004.

This is a smaller, popular version of the major book on all things medical.

J. G. Hardman and L. E. Limbird. *Goodman and Gilman's The Pharmacological Basis of Therapeutics.* McGraw-Hill, 2001.

This book provides very deep reading about medications, including how they work and how they are used.

J. M. Jellin, P. J. Gregory, et al. *Natural Medicines Comprehensive Database.* Therapeutic Research Faculty, 2007.

This book is the yearly publication of the database of the same name (see above) and it provides the last word on vitamins, supplements, and herbal products. However, it is expensive to buy the book, so look for a used or library copy.

Eric Kandel, J. H. Schwartz, and Thomas M. Jessell. *Principles of Neural Science.* McGraw-Hill, 2000.

This book is held in high esteem as a neuropsychology textbook.

PDR Staff, editors. *Physicians' Desk Reference.* Thompson PDR, 2007.

The *PDR* contains over three thousand pages of FDA-approved information on many prescription medications, written for physicians.

B. J. Sadock and V. A. Sadock. *Kaplan and Sadock's Comprehensive Textbook of Psychiatry.* Lippincott Williams & Wilkins, 2005.

Kaplan and Sadock's is the ultimate professional resource on psychiatry facts, theory, and treatment.

Andrew Steptoe, editor. *Depression and Physical Illness.* Cambridge University Press, 2006.

This book is difficult to read but contains a comprehensive collection of information about the complex interweaving of unipolar major depression and bodily illnesses, such as cancer and heart disease.

Some Popular Books on Depression

These popular books address different aspects of depression from different viewpoints. They may give you some new ideas.

Aaron Beck, J. Rush, B. Shaw, and G. Emery. *Cognitive Therapy of Depression*. Guilford Press, 1979.

This is an instructive book on cognitive therapy by the man who helped popularize it.

Wes Burgess, MD, PhD. *The Bipolar Handbook*. Avery/Penguin, 2006.

Wes Burgess, MD, PhD. *The Bipolar Handbook for Children, Adolescents, and Families*. Avery/Penguin, 2008.

David D. Burns. *Feeling Good: The New Mood Therapy*. Harper, 1999.

David Burns has written a very popular book on depression and what to do about it.

William J. Knaus and Albert Ellis. *The Cognitive Behavioral Workbook for Depression: A Step-by-Step Program*. New Harbinger, 2006.

Albert Ellis was a great innovator in the world of psychology. This book explains his methods and their modern application in cognitive behavioral therapy.

ICON Health Publications Staff. *Major Depression: A Medical Dictionary, Bibliography, and Annotated Research Guide to Internet References*. ICON Health Publications, 2000.

This volume provides access to lots of information on unipolar major depression.

J. Mark, G. Williams, John Teasdale Zindel, V. Segal, Jon Kabat-Zinn. *The Mindful Way through Depression*. Guilford Press, 2007.

This popular book discusses the concept "mindfulness," said to be a Western interpretation of Eastern meditation practices.

Practical Philosophical Books Relevant for Depression

Depression often stimulates a lot of thinking about your past, your future, and how to get what you want in your life. These books may provide you with some support and help and give you an opportunity to replace your negative thoughts with some constructive, positive ones.

Renford Bambrough, editor. *The Philosophy of Aristotle*. New American Library, 1963.

>   Aristotle can speak loudly to depression sufferers. His is an attempt to make sense of the world through observation and understanding, where clear thinking can separate empty theory from the truth. Could he have been depressed?

J. Krishnamurti. *Commentaries on Living*. First, Second and Third Series. Penguin Books, 2006.

>   These readable volumes address a variety of practical issues while demonstrating a healthy philosophy of insight and objectivity.

Richard McKeon, editor. *Introduction to Aristotle*. The New Modern Library, 1947.

>   This classic contains more of Aristotle's practical, organized, and logical thinking. After being taught by Plato, Aristotle developed his own philosophic style that evolved into what we now call science.

Red Pine, translator. *The Zen Teaching of Bodhidharma*. North Point Press, 1989.

>   History says that when Bodhidharma reached enlightenment, he came down the mountain and taught Zen at the Shaolin monastery there. When the modern generation of Shaolin monks was asked about Bodhidharma, they looked back in their ancient records and told us that their ancestors thought that Bodhidharma was a big pest.

Paul Reps, editor. *Zen Flesh, Zen Bones*. Penguin Books, 2000.
Reps has collected material from three books and an article from *Gentry* magazine to illustrate Zen thought. If you are tired of struggling with the rigid, linear Western style of thinking, then you may find this book interesting.

Ludwig Wittgenstein. *Zettel*. Edited by G. E. M. Anscombe and G. H. Von Wright. University of California Press, 1970.
This is a very accessible volume of short thoughts by Wittgenstein on the philosophical outlook that he originated called logical positivism. Wittgenstein seems to have known depression well.

Prose and Poetry

When depression is holding you down, you need books that speak to the depressed soul. These are some wonderful choices.

E. E. Cummings. *95 Poems*. Liverwright Publishing, 2002.
In his small way, Cummings speaks to the depressed poet in all of us.

Lawrence Ferlinghetti. *Coney Island of the Mind*. New Directions, 1974.
Clever, amusing, and sometimes scary, Ferlinghetti has drunk deep at the well of emotion and, like his dog, has quite a tale to tell.

Jack Kerouac. *On the Road*. Penguin, 1999.
The Beat Generation speaks the language of depression. Ultimately, it's not what you say but the way that you say it.

Kenneth Koch. *The Collected Poems of Kenneth Koch*. Knopf Publishing Group, 2007.
Through all his obsessive details, Koch seems like a moviemaker whose camera is always pointed slightly away from the action, yet his fascination with words cuts through the limitations of language like a knife.

Sylvia Plath. *The Bell Jar*. Harper Perennial Modern Classics, 2002. This book outlines the experiences of a woman suffering with depression. For a variety of reasons, she was not given antidepressants, and she killed herself after writing this book.

Doctors' Criteria for a Major Depressive Episode

A. Five (or more) of the following symptoms have been present during the same 2-week period and represent a change from previous functioning; at least one of the symptoms is either (1) depressed mood or (2) loss of interest or pleasure.

(1) Depressed mood most of the day, nearly every day, as indicated by either subjective report (e.g., feels sad or empty) or observation made by others (e.g., appears tearful). In children and adolescents, can be irritable mood.

(2) Markedly diminished interest or pleasure in all, or almost all, activities most of the day, nearly every day (as indicated by either subjective account or observation made by others).

(3) Significant weight gain or loss when not dieting (e.g., a change of more than 5 percent of body weight in a month), or decrease or increase in appetite nearly every day.

(4) Insomnia or hypersomnia nearly every day

(5) Psychomotor agitation or retardation nearly every day (observable by others, not merely subjective feelings of restlessness or being slowed down).

(6) Fatigue or loss of energy nearly every day.

(7) Feelings of worthlessness or excessive or inappropriate guilt (which may be delusional) nearly every day (not merely self-reproach or guilt about being sick).

(8) Diminished ability to think or concentrate, or indecisiveness, nearly every day (either by subjective account or as observed by others).

(9) Recurrent thoughts of death (not just fear of dying), recurrent suicidal ideation without a specific plan, or a suicide attempt or a specific plan for committing suicide.

B. The symptoms do not meet criteria for a Bipolar Mixed Episode.

C. The symptoms cause clinically significant distress or impairment in social, occupational, or other important areas of functioning.

D. The symptoms are not due to the direct physiological effects of a substance (e.g., a drug of abuse, a medication) or a general medical condition (e.g., hypothyroidism).

E. The symptoms are not better accounted for by Bereavement, i.e., after the loss of a loved one, the symptoms persist for longer than 2 months or are characterized by marked functional impairment, morbid preoccupation with worthlessness, suicidal ideation, psychotic symptoms, or psychomotor retardation.

With Melancholic Features

A. Either of the following, occurring during the most severe period of the current episode:

(1) Loss of pleasure in all or almost all activities.

(2) Lack of reactivity to usually pleasurable stimuli (does not feel much better, even temporarily, when something good happens).

B. Three (or more) of the following:

(1) Distinct quality of depressed mood (i.e., the depressed mood is experienced as distinctly different from the kind of feeling experienced after the death of a loved one).

(2) Depression regularly worse in the morning.

(3) Early morning awakening (at least 2 hours before usual time of awakening)

(4) Marked psychomotor retardation or agitation.

(5) Significant anorexia or weight loss.

(6) Excessive or inappropriate guilt.

Appendix C

THE NATIONAL INSTITUTE OF MENTAL HEALTH'S SYMPTOMS OF GENERAL DEPRESSION AND PSYCHOSIS

Signs and symptoms of depression include:

- Lasting sad, anxious, or empty mood
- Feelings of hopelessness or pessimism
- Feelings of guilt, worthlessness, or helplessness
- Loss of interest or pleasure in activities once enjoyed, including sex
- Decreased energy, a feeling of fatigue or of being "slowed down"
- Difficulty concentrating, remembering, making decisions
- Restlessness or irritability
- Sleeping too much, or can't sleep
- Change in appetite and unintended weight loss or gain
- Chronic pain or other persistent bodily symptoms that are not caused by physical illness or injury
- Thoughts of death or suicide, or suicide attempts

A depressive episode is diagnosed if five or more of these symptoms last most of the day, nearly every day, for a period of two weeks or longer.

Common symptoms of psychosis include
Hallucinations: Hearing, seeing, or otherwise sensing the presence of
things not actually there
Delusions: false, strongly held beliefs (not influenced by logical
reasoning or explained by a person's usual cultural concepts)

Note: Reprinted with permission from: National Institute of Mental
Health. Bipolar disorder, www.nimh.nih.gov/publicat/bipolar.cfm,
Bethesda (MD): National Institute of Mental Health, National
Institutes of Health, US Department of Health and Human Services;
2001. Updated: 09/02/2005. NIH Publication No 3679. See
Appendix A, Resources, for contact information.

Appendix D

These worksheets will help you understand your unipolar major depression and speed your progress to your most normal, natural self.

PLEASANT EVENTS PROGRAM

Check all the activities you like to do or think you would like to do. Add your own favorites. Fill in the dates when you plan to do them. After you have completed each activity, circle the date to show that you are successfully following the program.

Things You Like to Do: Dates You Plan to Do Them:

	Mon.	Tues.	Wed.	Thurs.	Fri.	Sat.	Sun.
❑ Call a relative or friend	___	___	___	___	___	___	___
❑ Attend a concert	___	___	___	___	___	___	___
❑ Cook a nice meal	___	___	___	___	___	___	___
❑ Visit a museum	___	___	___	___	___	___	___
❑ Dance	___	___	___	___	___	___	___
❑ Play a game	___	___	___	___	___	___	___
❑ Work on an art project	___	___	___	___	___	___	___
❑ Go to a movie	___	___	___	___	___	___	___
❑ Have friends over	___	___	___	___	___	___	___
❑ Read a book or magazine	___	___	___	___	___	___	___
❑ Eat at a restaurant	___	___	___	___	___	___	___
❑ Fly a kite	___	___	___	___	___	___	___
❑ Attend a play	___	___	___	___	___	___	___
❑ Go bowling	___	___	___	___	___	___	___
❑ Watch a DVD	___	___	___	___	___	___	___
❑ Hike or camp	___	___	___	___	___	___	___
❑ Take photos	___	___	___	___	___	___	___
❑ Watch sports	___	___	___	___	___	___	___
❑ Go to the park	___	___	___	___	___	___	___
❑ Go to the library	___	___	___	___	___	___	___
❑ Go to the zoo	___	___	___	___	___	___	___
❑ Sing in the shower	___	___	___	___	___	___	___
❑ Get out in the sun	___	___	___	___	___	___	___

Things You Like to Do:	Dates You Plan to Do Them:
❑ Walk or run	— — — — — — —
❑ Listen to music	— — — — — — —
❑ Meditate	— — — — — — —
❑ Go for a drive	— — — — — — —
❑ Play a musical instrument	— — — — — — —
❑ Go out with friends	— — — — — — —
❑ Take a trip	— — — — — — —
❑ Visit a friend's home	— — — — — — —
❑ _____	— — — — — — —
❑ _____	— — — — — — —
❑ _____	— — — — — — —
❑ _____	— — — — — — —
❑ _____	— — — — — — —
❑ _____	— — — — — — —
❑ _____	— — — — — — —
❑ _____	— — — — — — —
❑ _____	— — — — — — —

LIFE ACTIVATION FRAMEWORK

What things made life more enjoyable this week? Think of other things you noticed and enjoyed. Check each day that you:

	Mon.	Tues.	Wed.	Thurs.	Fri.	Sat.	Sun.
Felt love for someone	❑	❑	❑	❑	❑	❑	❑
Looked at the sky	❑	❑	❑	❑	❑	❑	❑
Kissed someone	❑	❑	❑	❑	❑	❑	❑
Noticed you were relaxed	❑	❑	❑	❑	❑	❑	❑
Were a good listener	❑	❑	❑	❑	❑	❑	❑
Looked at the moon or stars	❑	❑	❑	❑	❑	❑	❑
Read a book or magazine	❑	❑	❑	❑	❑	❑	❑
Went outdoors	❑	❑	❑	❑	❑	❑	❑
Wore favorite clothes	❑	❑	❑	❑	❑	❑	❑
Looked forward to something	❑	❑	❑	❑	❑	❑	❑
Told someone you love them	❑	❑	❑	❑	❑	❑	❑
Listened to music	❑	❑	❑	❑	❑	❑	❑
Learned something	❑	❑	❑	❑	❑	❑	❑
Admired someone	❑	❑	❑	❑	❑	❑	❑
Received a compliment	❑	❑	❑	❑	❑	❑	❑
Ate a favorite food	❑	❑	❑	❑	❑	❑	❑
Received help	❑	❑	❑	❑	❑	❑	❑
Told a joke or story	❑	❑	❑	❑	❑	❑	❑
Drank a beverage and relaxed	❑	❑	❑	❑	❑	❑	❑
Watched the sunrise or sunset	❑	❑	❑	❑	❑	❑	❑
Made someone happy	❑	❑	❑	❑	❑	❑	❑
Had a moment of feeling good	❑	❑	❑	❑	❑	❑	❑
Solved a problem	❑	❑	❑	❑	❑	❑	❑
Heard a joke or story	❑	❑	❑	❑	❑	❑	❑
Played with a child or pet	❑	❑	❑	❑	❑	❑	❑
Played a game	❑	❑	❑	❑	❑	❑	❑
Enjoyed working out	❑	❑	❑	❑	❑	❑	❑
Enjoyed being with others	❑	❑	❑	❑	❑	❑	❑

	Mon.	Tues.	Wed.	Thurs.	Fri.	Sat.	Sun.
Helped someone	☐	☐	☐	☐	☐	☐	☐
Said something interesting	☐	☐	☐	☐	☐	☐	☐
Were praised	☐	☐	☐	☐	☐	☐	☐
Felt happy	☐	☐	☐	☐	☐	☐	☐
Talked to a friend	☐	☐	☐	☐	☐	☐	☐
Gave thanks	☐	☐	☐	☐	☐	☐	☐
Wrote something for pleasure	☐	☐	☐	☐	☐	☐	☐
Received a kiss	☐	☐	☐	☐	☐	☐	☐
Enjoyed a sunny day	☐	☐	☐	☐	☐	☐	☐
Received an "I love you"	☐	☐	☐	☐	☐	☐	☐
Played some music	☐	☐	☐	☐	☐	☐	☐
Saw a picture or photo	☐	☐	☐	☐	☐	☐	☐
Showed someone you care	☐	☐	☐	☐	☐	☐	☐
Noticed a tree or flower	☐	☐	☐	☐	☐	☐	☐
Had a meaningful conversation	☐	☐	☐	☐	☐	☐	☐
Heard some good news	☐	☐	☐	☐	☐	☐	☐
Went to a place you like	☐	☐	☐	☐	☐	☐	☐
Felt powerful	☐	☐	☐	☐	☐	☐	☐
Touched someone you care for	☐	☐	☐	☐	☐	☐	☐
Met a new person	☐	☐	☐	☐	☐	☐	☐
Did something nice for yourself	☐	☐	☐	☐	☐	☐	☐
Admired an animal or child	☐	☐	☐	☐	☐	☐	☐
Created something good	☐	☐	☐	☐	☐	☐	☐
Had a friendly conversation	☐	☐	☐	☐	☐	☐	☐
Received a friendly comment	☐	☐	☐	☐	☐	☐	☐
Took a pleasant walk	☐	☐	☐	☐	☐	☐	☐
Said something clever	☐	☐	☐	☐	☐	☐	☐
Recalled a pleasant memory	☐	☐	☐	☐	☐	☐	☐
Had a new thought	☐	☐	☐	☐	☐	☐	☐
Received a present	☐	☐	☐	☐	☐	☐	☐
Did something healthy	☐	☐	☐	☐	☐	☐	☐

EMOTION CHECKLIST

Look at the Emotion Checklist, and mark every word that describes how you feel right now. Note that the emotions start out mild and become stronger as you go to the bottom of each list. Check your emotions every few days, and keep your old checklists so you can compare your feelings from day to day.

HAPPY EMOTIONS   SAD EMOTIONS

Weakest	❒ hopeful	❒ delighted	❒ solemn	❒ pessimistic
–	❒ encouraged	❒ joyful	❒ gloomy	❒ let-down
–	❒ pleased	❒ excited	❒ sad	❒ discouraged
–	❒ self-confident	❒ uplifted	❒ blue	❒ disillusioned
–	❒ glad	❒ inspired	❒ melancholy	❒ heartbroken
–	❒ happy	❒ exuberant	❒ sorrowful	❒ hopeless
–	❒ cheerful	❒ thrilled	❒ grim	❒ defeated
–	❒ bright	❒ exhilarated	❒ dismal	❒ desperate
–	❒ sunny	❒ ecstatic	❒ anguished	❒ doomed
Strongest	❒ enthusiastic	❒ high	❒ tormented	❒ lost

ANXIOUS EMOTIONS   ANGRY EMOTIONS

Weakest	❒ tense	❒ cautious	❒ flustered	❒ displeased
–	❒ uneasy	❒ apprehensive	❒ impatient	❒ perturbed
–	❒ fidgety	❒ worried	❒ frustrated	❒ annoyed
–	❒ edgy	❒ fearful	❒ exasperated	❒ brooding
–	❒ anxious	❒ afraid	❒ grumpy	❒ angry
–	❒ restless	❒ scared	❒ ill-tempered	❒ incensed
–	❒ jittery	❒ alarmed	❒ irritable	❒ furious
–	❒ jumpy	❒ terrified	❒ irritated	❒ enraged
–	❒ keyed-up	❒ panicked	❒ aggravated	❒ boiling
Strongest	❒ agitated	❒ hysterical	❒ indignant	❒ explosive

Index

About the Author

Wes Burgess, MD, PhD, is a practicing Los Angeles psychiatrist specializing in the diagnosis and treatment of mood disorders. He is the author of the successful books *The Bipolar Handbook* and *The Bipolar Handbook for Children, Teens, and Families*. A featured commentator on National Public Radio (NPR) and network television, he received his training at Stanford University Medical Center and has taught at Stanford, UCLA, and other major universities.

Cheryl Rizzo